Transforming Defensiveness

Transforming Defensiveness

A Guidebook for Rewriting Our Stories & Reclaiming Connection

ANDREA L. DOTTOLO

Copyright © 2026 by John Wiley & Sons, Inc. All rights reserved, including rights for text and data mining and training of artificial intelligence technologies or similar technologies.

Published by John Wiley & Sons, Inc., Hoboken, New Jersey.

No part of this publication may be reproduced, stored in a retrieval system, or transmitted in any form or by any means, electronic, mechanical, photocopying, recording, scanning, or otherwise, except as permitted under Section 107 or 108 of the 1976 United States Copyright Act, without either the prior written permission of the Publisher, or authorization through payment of the appropriate per-copy fee to the Copyright Clearance Center, Inc., 222 Rosewood Drive, Danvers, MA 01923, (978) 750-8400, fax (978) 750-4470, or on the web at www.copyright.com. Requests to the Publisher for permission should be addressed to the Permissions Department, John Wiley & Sons, Inc., 111 River Street, Hoboken, NJ 07030, (201) 748-6011, fax (201) 748-6008, or online at http://www.wiley.com/go/permission.

The manufacturer's authorized representative according to the EU General Product Safety Regulation is Wiley-VCH GmbH, Boschstr. 12, 69469 Weinheim, Germany, e-mail: Product_Safety@wiley.com.

Trademarks: Wiley and the Wiley logo are trademarks or registered trademarks of John Wiley & Sons, Inc. and/or its affiliates in the United States and other countries and may not be used without written permission. All other trademarks are the property of their respective owners. John Wiley & Sons, Inc. is not associated with any product or vendor mentioned in this book.

Limit of Liability/Disclaimer of Warranty: While the publisher and the authors have used their best efforts in preparing this work, including a review of the content of the work, neither the publisher nor the authors make any representations or warranties with respect to the accuracy or completeness of the contents of this work and specifically disclaim all warranties, including without limitation any implied warranties of merchantability or fitness for a particular purpose. Certain AI systems have been used in the creation of this work. No warranty may be created or extended by sales representatives, written sales materials or promotional statements for this work. The fact that an organization, website, or product is referred to in this work as a citation and/or potential source of further information does not mean that the publisher and authors endorse the information or services the organization, website, or product may provide or recommendations it may make. This work is sold with the understanding that the publisher is not engaged in rendering professional services. The advice and strategies contained herein may not be suitable for your situation. You should consult with a specialist where appropriate. Further, readers should be aware that websites listed in this work may have changed or disappeared between when this work was written and when it is read. Neither the publisher nor authors shall be liable for any loss of profit or any other commercial damages, including but not limited to special, incidental, consequential, or other damages.

For general information on our other products and services or for technical support, please contact our Customer Care Department within the United States at (800) 762-2974, outside the United States at (317) 572-3993 or fax (317) 572-4002.

Wiley also publishes its books in a variety of electronic formats. Some content that appears in print may not be available in electronic formats. For more information about Wiley products, visit our web site at www.wiley.com.

Library of Congress Cataloging-in-Publication Data

Names: Dottolo, Andrea L. author
Title: Transforming defensiveness : a guidebook for rewriting our stories & reclaiming connection / Andrea L. Dottolo.
Description: Hoboken, New Jersey : Wiley, [2026] | Includes bibliographical references and index.
Identifiers: LCCN 2025054125 (print) | LCCN 2025054126 (ebook) | ISBN 9781394296798 paperback | ISBN 9781394296828 adobe pdf | ISBN 9781394296804 epub
Subjects: LCSH: Defensiveness (Psychology) | Defense mechanisms (Psychology)
Classification: LCC BF175.5.D44 D68 2026 (print) | LCC BF175.5.D44 (ebook)
LC record available at https://lccn.loc.gov/2025054125
LC ebook record available at https://lccn.loc.gov/2025054126

Cover Design: Wiley
Cover Image: © wildpixel/Getty Images

Set in 9/13pt Ubuntu by Straive, Pondicherry, India

Contents

Acknowledgments	**vii**

Transforming Defensiveness: A Guidebook for Rewriting Our Stories & Reclaiming Connection   **1**
Andrea L. Dottolo

The Classroom	2
The Professor Arrives	2
Opening Moves	3
The Discussion Begins	4
More Questions	5
Introduction	5

Chapter 1: What Is Defensiveness?   **12**

Defining Defensiveness?	13
Learning Outcomes	25
What is the Purpose of Defensiveness?	25
The Change Triangle	28
Coping vs. Defensiveness	32
Summary	34

Chapter 2: Why Do We Sometimes Feel Defensive?   **35**

In-Group Bias	37
Intersectionality	41
Stereotypes & Discrimination	44
Belief in a Just World	47
Investment in the Status Quo	52
Fear of Change	55
Shame	57
Summary	59

Chapter 3: Recognizing Defensiveness   **60**

Denial	61
Avoidance	65
Minimization	67
Rationalization	70
Blaming the Victim	72
Projection	78
Repression	80
Regression	83
Anger	85
Protectiveness of Others	87
Displacement	90
Reaction Formation	91
Undoing	93
Distancing	95
Religious or Biological Law	98
Sublimation	101
Competing Victimization	103
Intellectualization	105
Humor	107
Summary	109

Chapter 4: So Now What? What Can We Do?   **110**

Focus On You	111
Focus On Others	117
Focus On Groups	121
Summary	126

Chapter 5: Conclusion 128

Myths About Defensiveness 129
Defensiveness in a
    Digital Age 140
Defensiveness in Today's
    Political Climate 143
Defensiveness and
    Artificial Intelligence:
    A Special Case 147
Narrative Defense and the
    Power of Storytelling 147
Strategies to Reduce
    Defensiveness in a Polarized,
    Digital World 150
More Ideas On How to Use
    This Book 153
Final Thoughts 156
Where to Go From Here 157
Future Directions 157

References 159

Index 180

Acknowledgments

This book is a culmination of my teaching and learning since my first year in graduate school, a few decades ago now. It is challenging to express gratitude for all those who have influenced my thinking along the way. As I have finished this manuscript, my own personal defenses have been deeply tested by life's challenges. I am overwhelmed at the support of my family and friends, who have provided words, compassion, understanding, space, and safety.

I could not conceive of how the evolution of this work could have happened without a cadre of peeps.

Many thanks to Megan Sumeracki, whose strategic thinking and pulling strings was pivotal. Sarah Tillery, my heart friend, has been my rock of support and strength, teaching me to unlearn, relearn, and try again. Diana Cutaia continued to offer to fly me places for friendship and renewal. Barb Anderson escaped death and remained as loyal and raucous as ever. Erika Gasser and Jon Barber provide warmth, laughter, and trusted counsel. Thank-you to Morgan Wall and Becca Longfellow for understanding what matters—hair. Sakiko Mori continues to teach me about safety, listening, and letting go. Randi Kim and Beth Lewis are not only trusted colleagues, but provided actual space for all of it. Thank-you to Pat Colabufo, whose magical presence spreads fairy dust wherever she goes.

My family has always been especially supportive and encouraging of my education. I thank my parents, Anthony and Carol Dottolo, for teaching me to value lifelong learning. My mother has been my writing partner and consultant since childhood, and she has read every word of this book, offering feedback, reactions, and a keen editing eye. My father has believed I could. My sister, Danielle Conroy, and her family, Patrick and Trey Conroy, have redefined our family. Emileen Butler's unwavering support is deeply known. Denise Faneuff has ushered an appreciated microscopic examination of defensiveness with patience and skill, and her voice about what it means to be gentle shapes my work in many ways.

And to Sandy McEvoy, whose presence has had a profound impact on each draft, iteration, and milestone of this book, my work, and over half of my life.

I thank the folks at Wiley for their help and guidance, especially Laura Pople and Janaki Kumudam Gothandaraman.

ChatGPT helped organize my ideas, suggest alternative phrasing for complex concepts, develop ideas for case studies and examples, and improve clarity and conciseness throughout the writing process. All AI-generated content was carefully reviewed, edited, and approved. The final analysis, conclusions, and interpretations represent my views and expertise. I take full responsibility for the content and accuracy of this work. In the end, it's the words that matter.

Transforming Defensiveness: A Guidebook for Rewriting Our Stories & Reclaiming Connection

By Andrea L. Dottolo

Transforming Defensiveness: A Guidebook for Rewriting Our Stories & Reclaiming Connection, First Edition. Andrea L. Dottolo.
© 2026 John Wiley & Sons, Inc. All rights reserved, including rights for text and data mining and training of artificial intelligence technologies or similar technologies.
Published 2026 by John Wiley & Sons, Inc.

THE CLASSROOM

The classroom is hot and steamy. It's the first day of the fall semester, though it feels like mid-July in the tropics. Outside, the sun blazes over the quad, where first-years clutch orientation maps and iced coffees. Inside, the air conditioner sputters, issuing a steady stream of noise, providing little relief.

The classroom is packed—thirty students, arranged in rows, facing forward. The chairs are old and wobbly. Some students shift uncomfortably. A few wear hoodies despite the heat, maybe for comfort, maybe for armor. Most have their eyes fixed downward, locked into their phones as if submerged in some digital lifeboat.

There are headphones, earbuds, smartwatches blinking. Two athletic-looking guys in the back lean in toward each other, whispering low. One chews on a protein bar wrapper. A student with purple hair sits near the front, expression unreadable behind black eyeliner. A few rows back, someone with periwinkle hair twirls a pen between their fingers, brows furrowed in concentration or boredom—impossible to tell. Another student scribbles something in the margins of a thick spiral notebook. There's a man in military fatigues near the door, seated ramrod straight, his backpack squared on the floor. A wide range of ages is represented—some students fresh faced and wide eyed, others carrying with them the evidence of experiences of a life lived.

THE PROFESSOR ARRIVES

At exactly 11:52 AM—eight minutes before the hour—a woman strides into the room. She is short, but walks like she owns the floor, every step deliberate. The kind of person who's learned to stretch her presence to fill the space she needs.

She reaches the podium in under ten seconds, plopping a large tote bag with a thunk onto the side table. From it, she pulls a water bottle, a battered folder, and a sleek tablet. Her outfit is calculated armor—tailored black slacks, a steel-gray blouse, and low-heeled black shoes. She'd spent far too long last night debating between this and a softer navy cardigan ensemble, finally choosing this more severe look. It was a kind of silent signal: Take me seriously.

Despite her calm, she can feel a familiar tightness under her ribs. That first-day blend of anticipation and low-grade panic. Even after all these years of teaching, that feeling never fully goes away. But she's learned to welcome it—it keeps her alert, honest.

She surveys the room. A sea of strangers.

"Hi everyone," she says, voice warm, measured. "I'm Dr. Felix. Welcome."

OPENING MOVES

After the usual housekeeping—syllabus highlights, office hours, digital platforms, a brief chuckle about the faulty A/C—she pivots.

"OK," she says, sliding her glasses up her nose. "Let's move on to the material for today, which is especially important because it will serve as a foundation for the rest of the course."

She clicks to a slide with a simple title: Exploring Defensiveness.

She speaks evenly, watching the room.

"Psychology as a discipline is interested in understanding thoughts, feelings, and behaviors. Some emotions feel good to us—joy, pride, relief. Others, not so much—shame, anger, fear. Most of us weren't raised in environments that encouraged us to examine those hard feelings. Sometimes we were told that having these feelings is weak. Or dangerous. Or that we should just 'get over it.' Sound familiar?"

A few heads nod. Someone in the back scoffs under their breath.

"In this class," she continues, "we're going to explore how identity and power shape the way we think, feel, and act. That means we will be talking about race, gender, sexuality, class, disability, and more. These aren't abstract topics—they live in our bodies and in our relationships. So it's natural that we might feel … uncomfortable. Confused. Defensive."

She scans the room again. One student shifts visibly in their seat, pulling their hoodie tighter around their body. Another, an older woman with silver-streaked braids, gives a slow nod. The guy with his legs wide, arms crossed, doesn't budge, but his jaw tenses.

"You all read the assignment I sent on defensiveness, right?" she asks.

A few students murmur yes. Others glance at each other. A hand rises halfway, then hesitates.

"Well," she says, smiling gently, "let's start there. Today we will spend time reviewing what you learned and addressing any questions you have about defensiveness. Who would like to go first?"

THE DISCUSSION BEGINS

A pause.

Then the girl with the periwinkle hair slowly raises her hand.

"I guess I'll go," she says. Her voice is soft, but clear. "The article made me kind of mad. It said that when people get defensive, it's usually not because they're actually being attacked—but because they feel exposed. That hit hard."

Several students look up. Dr. Felix nods.

"That's a very common reaction," she says. "And it makes sense. No one likes feeling vulnerable. What did you do when you noticed that feeling?"

"I ... kinda wanted to stop reading," the girl admits. "Like, I told myself the author was being preachy. But then I realized that was exactly what she meant by defensiveness."

A few chuckles. The tension in the room softens, just slightly.

A student in the third row raises his hand. He's wearing a track jacket, his hair neatly parted.

"So, like ... is defensiveness always bad?" he asks. "I mean, what if someone really is being unfair to you?"

"Great question," Dr. Felix says, nodding. "Defensiveness is not bad. It's protective. It's your psyche saying: 'I don't feel safe right now.' The question is—what is it protecting you from? And how can we tell the difference between justified self-advocacy ... and shutting down because of discomfort?"

Another hand shoots up, this time from a young Black woman near the windows.

"What if we've always had to be defensive?" she asks. "Like, if the world keeps trying to define you or erase you, how are you supposed to lower your guard?"

Dr. Felix meets her gaze.

"That's another excellent question. And it's something we'll unpack throughout the course. For people who've experienced marginalization, defensiveness isn't just psychological—it can be a form of survival. But even survival strategies can have a cost. Our work is to examine when we're using them, why, and whether they still serve us."

The student nods slowly, considering.

MORE QUESTIONS

Now the room begins to stir. More questions follow.
    "Can you be defensive without realizing it?"
    "How do you talk to someone who gets defensive every time you bring up race or gender?"
    "Are men more defensive than women?"
    "What if I'm worried I'll say the wrong thing and get labeled as ignorant?"
    "How do you know if you're the one with privilege? Like, I've had a hard life too."
    Dr. Felix listens carefully to each question, affirming the vulnerability behind them. She knows these questions aren't just about theory—they're about identity, belonging, and the fear of being misunderstood.
    "We're not here to shame each other," she says. "We're here to learn. Together. That means we'll make mistakes. And that's OK. What matters is what we do after we make them."
    She looks around the room again. The skeptical eyes have softened, just a bit. The crossed arms have relaxed. The room, though still hot, has begun to feel—almost—open.

INTRODUCTION

That classroom conversation was just the beginning. In the real world, outside the structure of lectures and textbooks, defense mechanisms do not arrive neatly labeled. They show up in arguments, in silence, in quick tempers, and in deflected compliments. They shape relationships, communication, and even self-worth—often without our awareness.
    This guidebook is a continuation of that first class. This book is about theory and practice, about recognizing defensiveness in yourself and others. It is about learning how to respond—not react. It is about trading your armor for insight, clarity, and connection.
    You might be wondering: What is a guidebook about defensiveness? This might sound confusing, scary, or may not sound like it might be useful to you in your life. Many of us might deny that we even need this book, or that we react to certain situations in our lives in defensive ways. Or you might be thinking: What is defensiveness, anyway? Why does it matter to know about defensiveness? Who cares? You might be thinking that defensive reactions

are only limited to physical behaviors, such as punching someone or overtly aggressive acts. While bodily reactions to threats certainly count as defensive behaviors, our brains have nuanced and sophisticated ways of protecting ourselves that are not just obviously physical.

Here is some good news: You won't have to look very hard to find defensiveness. It's everywhere. Basically, defensiveness is a response to threat, or ways that we defend ourselves from what we perceive as an attack, or a kind of danger. Sometimes those responses are conscious—we know we are doing it. Other times, we are not aware that we feel threatened, or that we are taking a position of protection or fighting back.

For example, when people ask what I do for a living, they often react defensively to the fact that I am a professor of psychology. Sometimes they look visibly uncomfortable and just look the other way, or change the topic, *avoiding* any further conversation about it. Sometimes they might ask, "Can you read my mind? Can you tell me what my dream means?" When I explain that I cannot read minds, or that I am not a clinician, they refuse to believe me, as if I am just hiding something (this is *denial*). Or, they might announce, "oh, so you must analyze everything all the time!"

Similarly, when people find out that I also teach gender & women's studies, I have had people (sometimes men) say, "Oh really? Let me tell you everything you need to know about women." Or, people have responded, "so you study cooking and sewing?" And then there is the reaction of being asked, "What about men's studies?" All of these can be considered as defensive reactions, as these individuals may have interpreted my area of expertise as scary, confusing, or upsetting to them in some way.

It is a goal of this book to identify defensive reactions, including thoughts, feelings, and behaviors, and to understand how those reactions affect us and our relationships. In our modern culture, technology, immigration, the economy, and the dynamics of globalization require us to learn strategies that will enable us to successfully interact with many different people. This influences how we work, learn, socialize, shop, love, and self-identify, just to name a few. In order to successfully navigate a shifting social terrain, we need to investigate some of the ways in which we respond to new situations and people, especially when we might feel uncomfortable. Sitting with discomfort can be challenging and difficult, but the rewards of getting to know ourselves and others better while improving our relationships can be worth it. Similarly, as we understand our responses to these new circumstances, we can become more aware of our own internal dynamics. This awareness is the first step toward change and success. Being "successful" does not only mean making money, getting a job, sustaining relationships with friends, family, and coworkers, but also mean offering respect, dignity, and compassion to ourselves and others.

Words matter. I repeat this mantra with myself, my students, and colleagues as a way to remind us that language is central to our lives. The way we speak to ourselves and others has tremendous effects on our world—on our physical and mental health; on our safety, agency, power, thoughts, feelings; on what we can know and how we can come to know it. Words shape our realities. Our stories—the stories we tell ourselves and others—are a central way in which we make meaning of our world.

As our political, social, and economic environment changes over time, understanding our thoughts, feelings, and behaviors remains important. Scholars and philosophers have been writing and thinking about this topic for centuries (Curzuer, 2012; Gallucci, 2000). More importantly, we continue to interact with new people, ideas, requirements, and responsibilities that shape how we understand ourselves and each other. Sometimes these changes feel like they are happening faster than we can keep up with, for example, in the domain of technology and artificial intelligence or AI. Other times it might feel like we are decades behind what should be necessary improvements, say, with infrastructure or education. Exploring how we might react in order to facilitate understanding, growth, and productivity will always be a necessary skill to any discipline, any profession, and any social situation.

Who I Am and Why I'm Doing This ...

Let me begin by telling you a little bit about me and why I am writing this book. I learned about defense mechanisms when I took my first introductory psychology course. We learned about Sigmund Freud (1894) who wrote about the human psyche and is considered to be the founder of psychoanalysis. I was fascinated. I wanted to learn more about his life and theories. When I learned about Freud's writings about defense mechanisms, I had one of those "a-ha" moments, as there were finally words to label experiences that I had and witnessed. My education continues to be a string of those moments, all of which I find exhilarating, when I realize someone else has written down a thought I have had, or an experience that I could not name. Those moments of understanding can be healing, helping me to feel less alone, and validate my thoughts and feelings. In an instant, I realized that Freud (and others) has observed, noticed, or been curious about something I never knew how to explain. Suddenly, I could better understand what was happening in my family, at school, in my friendships, and most of all, inside of me. Once I finished that first class, I knew I wanted to keep studying psychology.

I continued to earn graduate degrees in psychology and gender & women's studies. While in graduate school, I was a teaching assistant and also taught my own courses. I learned quickly that not everyone was as eager as I was to learn about topics covered in my courses, such as injustice, oppression, and suffering. These topics incited a variety of reactions in my students, such as fear, sadness, helplessness, and anger. I knew that we all needed some tools in order to navigate the challenging material of the course. The work over the next 25 years in both my teaching and research is how this book came to be.

Now I am a professor of psychology and gender & women's studies, and I teach courses about identities, especially questions about how we know who we are in relation to other individuals and groups. In particular, my courses focus on topics such as gender, race, social class, sexuality, and other social identities. At the beginning of each course, I have found it useful to equip students with information and tools to help them navigate what might be difficult conversations. Students often have strong feelings and beliefs about these topics and might find themselves in conflict with other students, the course material, or even within themselves as they try to negotiate multiple perspectives.

Perhaps reading about my training and expertise might evoke feelings of defensiveness for you, as these labels around race, class, gender, and sexuality can have various meanings to different people. Furthermore, these words and titles can shift in their meaning and cause confusion, angst, anger, and fear. Some of the words and labels related to these ideas can cause prejudice and discrimination and are seen as taboo. One of the intentions of this book is to clarify some of the confusion around these terms and help us to confront and better understand not only their meanings, but also our reaction to them. In doing so, we might be better able to communicate about them.

This might be the first time you are considering these topics or having these conversations. Or, you may have some experience with this content, in job training, classrooms, and overall life experiences. Sometimes these conversations can feel frustrating and disappointing for a few reasons. Often it might feel like you are being lectured, scolded, or just given information that you are "supposed to know." This guidebook is intended to be an interactive experience, offering some opportunities for you to reflect and engage with conversations with others. Frequently, people use cliches that are vague and feel empty, leaving us feeling confused. For example, you might hear phrases like "follow the golden rule," or "make sure everyone has a seat at the table," but without any practical strategies on how to make that happen in your own workplace or relationships.

This guidebook is grounded in scholarship, with each section offering explanations, examples, and exercises for you to consider. These pages offer you opportunities to reflect on your own experiences, learn about how researchers have come to understand defensiveness, explore some concrete examples, and apply some new tools to your relationships. My professional training and entire career have been devoted to developing ways to understand, practice, and implement these topics into my scholarship and teaching. In other words, this information is not simply my opinion, but instead rooted in evidence-based research and expertise. Over the years, other faculty, schools, organizations, and businesses have requested that I present this material to their teams to help them navigate their own learning and work contexts. In response, I have developed a workshop, and now this guidebook, to appeal to a broader audience in a variety of situations.

Why Should You Read This Book?

You may choose to be reading this book, or you may be required to engage with this material with varying levels of interest or motivation. You might be reading this for a class, a training, or for your own interest. You should read this book if you:

1. Want to learn more about yourself and your relationships
2. Seek to create change within individuals, communities, and institutions
3. Want to just get through a required class or training
4. Work in the "helping" professions such as nursing, teaching, counseling, and social work and would like to be more able to create a more accepting and understanding environment in your job
5. Recognize "us" vs. "them" dynamics in our culture and seek to understand and overcome defensive behavior in yourself and others

6. Work in sales and want to know more about people in order to advance your career
7. Need to avoid offensive, inappropriate, and/or illegal behaviors in the workplace in order to protect you and your employers
8. Work with students of all ages

You might be reading this book because you are a student, or maybe an employee or professional getting ready to take a professional development training course. You might be worried about the content you will discuss, or even be dreading what you are about to face. This book is not the training itself. This book is intended to prepare you to have those conversations, to familiarize yourself with possible reactions that you and others might have.

Professionals who work with teams and group dynamics in a variety of capacities will also find this book useful, including mental health providers and clinicians. Coaches may use these exercises and activities to improve group coherence and strategies in sports. The contents of this book may open research lines, assist in the development of specific clinical skills, education, strategies for empowerment, and promote more effective and efficient communication.

The purpose of this workbook is to serve as a tool kit to define and explore defensiveness, as a way to provide language and understanding of our own reactions to challenging information. The exercises provided are designed to encourage self-examination and evaluation. Honest and critical self-awareness is the goal. I hope you explore and investigate some of the ways that defense mechanisms show up in your life to protect you. You might even recognize some of the reactions of your family and friends. Learning to understand our defenses helps us to recognize them in ourselves and others, hopefully with the intention of facilitating empathy, awareness, and productive communication.

How Should You Read and Use This Book?

Academics, practitioners, students, leaders, professionals, workers, employees, and anyone reading this book should feel free to use it as you see fit. I recommend that everyone read Chapter 1: What is defensiveness? After that, you might focus more or less on the theoretical explanations, depending on your need. You might pay close attention to some of the defense mechanisms and skip others. You might concentrate on one or more of the exercises in various ways. All of the exercises are intended for personal reflection, so that if you choose to read the book from beginning to end, it could serve as a singular, self-contained guide. However, the exercises might become journaling activities or used for group discussions. Or, perhaps individuals work on the exercises together in pairs or small groups. They might be used as assignments, or tasks for completion for some kind of credit at your school, workplace, or other settings. The exercises might be considered as prompts for longer writing assignments, encouraging the gathering of information about a specific defense mechanism for deeper exploration. Perhaps they are activities for therapy sessions, workplace training, or courses on a variety of topics. Basically, defensiveness can arise in any social situation, and in response to many different stimuli such as books, films, media, etc.

Chapter 1
What Is Defensiveness?

*T*he second day of class begins much like the first: hot, muggy, and vaguely tense. The air conditioner is now accompanied by a small desk fan that Dr. Felix has brought from her office, which only cools a two-foot radius around her podium. She's dressed today in loose linen pants and a dark blouse with sleeves she can roll. Still professional, but softer. She wants to look like a person, not just a professor.

There's already a low hum of conversation when she arrives. Fewer students are wearing headphones today. The purple-haired student—whose name she now knows is Lark—waves in recognition. The student in military fatigues gives a small nod. A few have copies of the syllabus printed out and highlighted. Dr. Felix notices and smiles inwardly. Signs of life.

Today's topic is identity. Before launching into theory, she opens with a question written on the board in red marker:

- "What does it mean to say: 'I know who I am'?
- And who gets to decide?"

Transforming Defensiveness: A Guidebook for Rewriting Our Stories & Reclaiming Connection, First Edition. Andrea L. Dottolo.
© 2026 John Wiley & Sons, Inc. All rights reserved, including rights for text and data mining and training of artificial intelligence technologies or similar technologies.
Published 2026 by John Wiley & Sons, Inc.

She gives them five minutes to write privately. After the timer buzzes, there's a long pause. Finally, a hand rises. It's Darius—the student who had asked about privilege on the first day. He's wearing a fitted black T-shirt and scuffed sneakers. His notebook is open, though his page is mostly blank.

"I guess I wrote something like ... 'I know who I am because I've lived my life.' But, like ... the world keeps trying to tell me I'm wrong. That I'm angry or threatening or lazy or whatever. So who gets to decide? I want it to be me. But it doesn't always feel like that."

There's a murmur of agreement. Dr. Felix nods. "That tension between self-definition and imposed identity is something many people experience. Especially those whose bodies or lives challenge the dominant narrative."

"Yeah, but ..." *another voice chimes in. It's Leah, an older student. She sits near the aisle, arms folded over her bag.* "What about when people use their own experiences to reject facts? Like—'that's just my truth'—but then say things that are racist or homophobic or flat-out wrong. Don't we have to draw a line?"

A low "mmm-hmm" echoes from someone nearby. Darius nods slowly.

"That's a critical distinction," *Dr. Felix says.* "Self-knowledge is powerful—but it doesn't exempt us from accountability. In this course, we'll practice both: honoring lived experience, *and* being willing to challenge the assumptions that experience might carry."

Lark raises their hand tentatively. "I keep thinking about how my identity has changed. Like—I used to think I was a straight girl. Now I'm nonbinary and queer. So ... which identity is the real me?"

Heads swivel. Dr. Felix walks toward them gently.

"Maybe all of them," *she says.* "Maybe none. Identity isn't a fixed point. It evolves, just like we do. The important thing is to stay curious."

Lark bites their lip and nods.

DEFINING DEFENSIVENESS?

Contemporary culture tells us that talking about issues around race, class, gender, and sexuality are "hot topics" and often "controversial." Many people tend to avoid these topics and find them uncomfortable or threatening. Some families even have rules, where they agree not to discuss politics or religion at the dinner table, as a way to avoid arguments and hurt feelings. When these "difficult dialogues" do happen sometimes, people express being "stuck," including feeling afraid, angry, paralyzed, and resentful. Others find it challenging to even name their experiences in these instances and describe a heavy, sinking sensation in their stomach, chest, or throat (Hendel, 2018; Hitchcock, 1984). These are typical responses to feeling threatened.

Psychologists describe some of these reactions as defense mechanisms (Wade & Tavris, 2012). A defense mechanism is a mental process intended to protect us from uncomfortable thoughts or feelings (Cramer, 1991). Defensive reactions can be understood as reasonable, understandable psychological responses to anything that is construed as a "threat" (David & Lyons-Ruth, 2005). Exploring the language of defensiveness can help us identify a threat and ask questions about why it feels threatening. This is especially important when we discuss topics that we were taught are supposed to be "normal" and "natural" (e.g., gender, race, class) and that questioning them might feel like a threat. For example, some people believe that there are only two sexes, male and female, and that it is part of the "natural" order, sometimes even rooted in religious ideas (Murray, 2008). For centuries, people have used the Bible to claim that slavery is "natural" and "normal" (Haynes, 2002). Eugenicists also claimed that white people are "naturally" more intelligent, using biology and skull measurements to support their unjust beliefs (Chitty, 2009). Race is still used in medicine in diagnosis, prognosis, and treatment guidelines, especially with regard to maternal health (Clarke et al., 2022). When your personal, familial, or traditional beliefs contradict new information or ideas, this can create internal moments of conflict where we can feel discomfort, fear, anxiety, anger, or some other negative emotion. These feelings can be clues that we feel threatened.

Source: abluecup /123 RF Photos.

Many forms of defensiveness are unconscious, which means that they function and appear outside of our awareness. They get activated when we are confronted with ideas that threaten our established belief system. These beliefs are preconceived, often based on cultural norms and values. Opposition to our convictions of "the way things should be" can create internal discord, anxiety, confusion, and ambivalence.

Sigmund Freud (1923), the early psychologist who wrote about defensiveness, used an analogy of an iceberg to understand the mind. He said that awareness or the conscious mind was like the "tip of the iceberg." This represents what we can see and know. Far below the surface of the water is the unconscious, which represents what we cannot access. It is outside of our awareness.

Source: BrandwayArt / Adobe Stock Photos.

Another common analogy used in psychology explains defensiveness. Imagine you're walking in the forest, and suddenly you come face to face with an angry bear. What happens? Your heart races. Your muscles tense. Your brain shouts: *"Danger! Get ready to fight or run!"*

Chapter 1: What Is Defensiveness?   **15**

This is your fight-or-flight response—your brain's way of protecting you when it senses a threat (Sapolsky, 2004). Now, let's say, instead of a bear, someone says something that hurts your feelings or makes you feel attacked, like "Why did you do it like that?" or "You're always so lazy." Even though it's not a bear, your brain might still react the same way—like you are in danger. You might feel a sudden urge to defend yourself, argue, or shut down. That's defensiveness.

Defensiveness is when we react quickly to protect ourselves emotionally—just like we would from that angry bear—even if the threat isn't physical (Gottman & Silver, 1999). Our brain doesn't always know the difference between physical danger and emotional danger. It just wants to keep us safe. But just like running from the bear might save you, defensiveness can sometimes help protect your feelings. However, if you're always defensive when talking to others, especially in relationships or friendships, it can actually cause more problems. People might feel like you're not listening or that you're blaming them (Nichols & Straus, 2021). So, next time you feel defensive, try to pause and ask yourself: "*Is this really a bear? Or is it just a hard conversation?*" That pause can help your brain calm down and let you respond more clearly and kindly.

Source: sirisak / Adobe Stock Photos.

The "angry bear" or threat might appear when talking about difficult topics, such as "diversity and inclusion," and the confusion and discomfort that might result. This is especially important where we explore issues or topics that cultural assumptions deem acceptable. Questioning them might feel like a threat. It is important to examine our moments of discomfort and anxiety, as they might indicate a place where we feel the need to protect, or that an "angry bear" might be in the room. The "bear" might be something we all agree is threatening, or that only some people think is dangerous, or perhaps you are the only person in the room who "sees the bear."

Psychologists have long studied how people react when they feel threatened. One of the most well-known ideas is the "fight-or-flight" response. This means that when someone feels scared or in danger, they may either fight back or try to escape (Cannon, 1929; McCarty, 2016). If you encounter the angry bear, you might get ready to fight it off or run as fast as you can. But over time, researchers have learned that there are more than just two ways people react. Another common reaction is "freeze," where a person becomes so overwhelmed by fear or stress that they cannot move or decide what to do. It's like feeling stuck or frozen in place (Vanderpool, 2021).

More recently, experts have added a fourth response called "fawn." This happens when someone tries to stay safe by being overly helpful or pleasing others, even if it means ignoring their own needs or feelings (Vanderpool, 2021). For example, a person might agree with something they don't actually believe just to avoid conflict. Fawning often involves contorting one's own needs and desires in the service of attending to others (Clayton, 2025). Fawning is a survival mechanism that requires denying your own feelings and experiences and shapeshifting into what others want from you.

These four responses—fight, flight, freeze, and fawn—help us understand how people react to danger, not just physical danger like a bear, but also emotional or social threats, like being yelled at or feeling judged. Even though these reactions can be useful and protective, people are complex, and our responses don't always fit neatly into one category. Sometimes, we may do a mix of these things, depending on the situation and how safe or unsafe we feel. In our daily lives, our "bears" might be criticism, rejection, or conflict—and the way we respond can inform how we've learned to protect ourselves.

Fight:

Source: Ethibaud / Wikimedia Commons / CC-BY SA 4.0.

Flight:

Source: Starscream / Wikimedia Commons / CC-BY SA 3.0.

Freeze:

Source: Madhur D'silva / Wikimedia Commons / Public Domain.

Fawn:

Source: Sapsiwai / Getty Images.

Our individual and collective responses to threats are based on our past experiences, some of which we share and some of which are unique to our personal histories. For example, if you work at a fast food restaurant earning minimum wage and a law is passed that raises taxes on people who make minimum wage, all of your co-workers might feel angry or scared at this

Chapter 1: What Is Defensiveness?   19

information, where everyone "sees the bear." However, when discussing issues of sexual violence in a classroom, perhaps only women or feminized people in that room "see the bear." People who are feminized are those (regardless of their sex) who adopt or are expected to adopt traits, behaviors, or roles traditionally associated with femininity (e.g., being nurturing, submissive, appearance focused), and/or those who present themselves in a more feminine way through clothing, makeup, voice, or mannerisms. Or, you are in a group where it appears that everyone is straight or heterosexual, including you, but someone tells a homophobic joke, and your brother is gay, whom you love. You might be the only person in that space who "sees the bear."

It is that moment, when discomfort and other negative emotions arise, that can be a clue that we feel threatened. This is a critical opportunity for learning, meriting further investigation and identification of the threat. It is important to remember that we *all* use defense mechanisms. They exist to protect us from threats, outside of our awareness, often under the surface of consciousness. Examining them in closer detail is not about blaming, or naming who is at fault, but instead about becoming aware of how they live inside us. The purpose of this exploration is to offer some specific and concrete strategies to address them.

To illustrate, imagine you are in a group where the topic of immigration comes up. In the room, unbeknownst to you, there are some immigrants, some children of immigrants, and some people whose ancestors have been living in the country for generations. Some people start saying that "immigrants don't belong here and should go back to their country." They might say that they are "taking our jobs," or are "criminals." Some others say that immigrants are valuable resources, most of whom are taxpayers, who are helpful to our economy and our country. Can you see how the "angry" bear might manifest itself in different ways inside this group? Or even as an observer of the conversation? Some people might not see a "bear" at all.

It is important to recognize that people are always carrying with them a constellation of identities, experiences, and connections that shape how they interpret the world, and many of these aspects are not immediately visible to others. While some characteristics that people often (incorrectly) assume may be perceived at a glance—such as race, gender, or age—other influential identities and experiences including sexuality, religion, social class, family history, or personal traumas, remain unseen. These invisible elements can deeply inform a person's sense of safety and belonging in any given moment, and they often influence how one responds to a comment, action, or joke. As described earlier, when someone hears a homophobic joke, the reaction may not simply be a matter of humor or taste; it may trigger a defensive or protective response rooted in personal identity, lived experience, or close relationships with others who are affected. Acknowledging the presence of these less visible but equally significant dimensions of identity early on helps create space for empathy and reminds us that every interaction takes place within a web of histories and contexts we cannot fully know. Naming this complexity upfront allows later examples to resonate more deeply since we will already understand that reactions are never just about what is seen on the surface.

Another example of an "angry bear" appears in the book *Knife* (2024) by Salman Rushdie when he writes about his attempted murder by a Muslim extremist. Rushdie had received death threats from Muslim extremists since the publishing of his book *The Satanic Verses* in 1988. Some Muslim fundamentalists interpreted Rushdie's book to be an "unholy" criticism of their religion. Over 30 years after this book was published, Rushdie was a victim of a knife attack when he was giving a talk at the Chautauqua Institute in New York. He was brutally stabbed over 15 times, losing an eye, sustaining life-threatening injuries by a 20-year-old man whose radical Islamic beliefs led to his attack. Being unable to actually engage with his assailant, he imagines an interview with the attacker. Rushdie (2024) wonders,

> I want to understand. This is my difficulty. The reasons you give don't seem strong enough to drive a young man, a young man who never was violent before, a young man who wasn't even very good at boxing, an amateur ... to drive such a man to sacrifice the rest of his life just to murder a stranger.
>
> *(p. 5)*

We might argue that an important piece of a response to Rushdie's challenge to understand, or the motivation for the attack, was based on an extreme defensiveness. In other words, the attacker's rage was fueled by his perception of Rushdie as a threat, as an "angry bear." In response, the attacker "fought back" against a person who delivered ideas he found threatening. While Rushdie (2024) keeps asking "Why?" he believes that his attacker would be unable to engage, refusing to answer his question, firmly grounded in the rigidity of his convictions. The attacker was unable to tolerate the existence of another point of view and responded to a perceived threat with violence. This is an extreme example, but not an uncommon reaction when we consider the violence and destruction caused worldwide by conflicting ideologies that are the cause of violence based on fear and anger (Rushdie, 2024).

Another "angry bear" might appear in a classroom. Imagine I am a new teacher in a 5th-grade classroom. I have a student who sits in the back of the classroom, falling asleep and not paying attention. Sometimes, when he should be working, he looks at his phone, talks to his classmates, doodles on his paper, and regularly doesn't do his homework. As the new teacher, I might feel angry, frustrated, and resentful toward him and his behavior. However, eventually I learn that his single parent works the night shift. The student is responsible for his younger siblings, getting them to school, and sometimes he doesn't have enough food. Perhaps this knowledge helps me feel less personally attacked, understanding that his behaviors are not about me. Perhaps I cannot imagine having his experience because my background was different, where I never wanted for breakfast. I learn that the broad spectrum of experiences in my classroom require me to ask more questions and to situate and understand my own feelings of defensiveness in a different way.

Another way to understand how defensiveness works is to shift our focus to how the brain works. The field of neuroscience, using scientific methods and advances in technology, is devoted to interpreting and discovering the complex workings of the brain. The front part of the brain, known as the prefrontal cortex, is responsible for rational thought and decision making (Hendel, 2018). We can think of this as a wise portion of the brain, sometimes referred to as our "*wizard* brain." We rely on this part of our brain to be calm, collected, thoughtful, and connected, responsible for planning, self-awareness, and impulse control (Hammond, 2014). When we feel scared or threatened, our limbic system is activated, which evaluates threats and strong emotions. It is a more primal part of our brain, sometimes referred to as our "*lizard* brain" (Troncale, 2014). When strong emotions, especially fear, come to the surface, our prefrontal cortex "goes offline," making it difficult to reason, think rationally, or react in a thoughtful way. This is when our automatic defensive responses such as fight, flight, freeze, and fawn get activated (Van der Kolk, 2014).

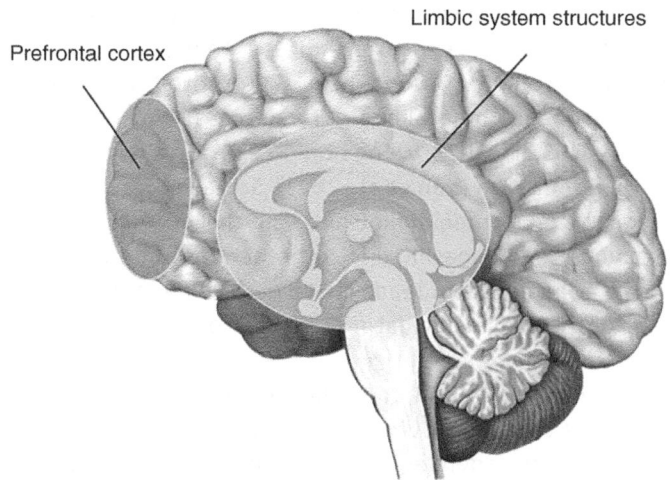

Learning to understand our defenses helps us to recognize them in ourselves and others, hopefully with the intention of facilitating awareness and constructive communication (Baker, 1980; Suyemoto & Hochman, 2021). Since awareness is the first step toward social change (Harro, 2000), identifying and labeling our responses is essential. In the moment, when someone displays defensiveness, we can reflect on not reacting with their *own* defensive response (which can be tricky). This guide will provide us with language and examples of responses we might rely upon in "difficult" discussions. For example, when someone claims that they are not homophobic because their "son is gay," it might be useful to highlight the ways in which we, all of us, are raised in a culture where we may unconsciously internalize homophobia to varying degrees.

In order to foster safer, more empathetic working relationships and to facilitate the application of this work, this book will allow the readers to select parts or all of the guidebook. If you are an academic or practitioner, I encourage you to read the sections that explain the theoretical explanations of defensiveness. Even if you are not an academic or practitioner, I hope you find these sections useful and meaningful. Some sections might be particularly relevant to different groups for various reasons.

One of the purposes of this guidebook is to prepare us for conversations about deeper, or "controversial" topics. The exercises can equip us with language and examples to help us consider some of the ways we might react. More importantly, this work is especially relevant in the wake of the COVID-19 pandemic. Research indicates that rates of anxiety and depression among college students have skyrocketed since the pandemic, further taxing students' mental health resources (Dixon et al., 2023; Lee et al., 2021; Ni & Jia, 2023; Wang et al., 2020). This might also be true of the general population (Kan et al., 2021). Social interactions and coping skills appear to have become diminished, and this book can serve as a practical resource for navigating difficult reactions and conversations. My experience as an educator leads me to believe people are hungry for guidance and assistance in navigating "difficult dialogues" in our current social climate.

Recently, conversations about race, class, gender, and sexuality have shifted in response to social movements such as #MeToo, Black Lives Matter, the Women's March, transgender, and queer liberation movements. While the need for diversity, equity, and inclusion efforts has increased, institutions are eliminating them (Candilis, 2023; Kraus et al., 2022). Government policies change over time regarding the support of addressing various social issues. Bracket and Stern (2024) name a more complicated landscape compared to just 30 years ago, including issues such as climate change, school shootings, digital technology, and social media.

All of these social conditions point to an ever-increasing need for *emotional intelligence*, which can be defined as "a set of skills contributing to the accurate appraisal of emotions in self and others and the effective regulation of emotion in self and others" (Salovey & Mayer, 1990). This refers to one's ability to recognize, identify, and control one's feelings (Goleman, 2005). Researchers have demonstrated that emotional intelligence contains all kinds of benefits, from educational achievement (Petrides et al., 2004) to job performance and satisfaction (Wong & Law, 2002).

McCoy (2024) discusses an extension of this concept called *emotional granularity*, or the ability to be specific and precise in labeling our feelings, which can help us feel better in both the short and long term. You can think about this as understanding your emotions, at the "granular" level, in a nuanced and fine-tuned way. McCoy (2024) explains how Smidt and Suvak (2015) reviewed the research on emotional granularity and found that "folks who could differentiate their emotions while experiencing intense distress were less likely to engage in potentially harmful coping strategies, such as binge drinking, lashing out at others, and hurting themselves." In addition, "people who describe and label their emotions more specifically have less severe episodes of anxiety and depression" (McCoy, 2024). This means that someone who is able to identify their feelings in specific ways, such as "sad," "scared," or "angry," is better able to cope and has more indicators of well-being than someone who says that they feel "bad" or "upset" (McCoy, 2024).

This book aims to improve upon our emotional intelligence and emotional granularity especially as they relate to defensiveness. If we, as individuals, and then perhaps collectively, gain more skills and knowledge about ourselves, we can improve our personal and professional relationships and productivity by minimizing harm and facilitating well-being.

LEARNING OUTCOMES

By the time you complete this guidebook, you will be able to:

1. Define defensiveness and defense mechanisms
2. Identify different forms of defensiveness in yourself and others
3. Describe some of the reasons why we get defensive
4. Critically reflect on your own defensive tendencies
5. Explore scenarios and situations that trigger defensiveness in yourself and others
6. Apply some strategies in addressing defensiveness to foster better communication

WHAT IS THE PURPOSE OF DEFENSIVENESS?

Now that we have explored what defensiveness *is*, we now shift to examining its *purpose*. This section focuses on the broad, foundational concepts behind how defensiveness operates. In other words, we'll explore overarching theoretical frameworks that explain the general purpose of our defenses, namely, to protect us from perceived threats. In contrast, Chapter 2 will shift to a more focused lens, examining the specific factors that lead people to become defensive in particular situations. There, we'll look at distinct emotional triggers, thought patterns, and specific types of defensiveness that help clarify why it can arise in real-life contexts. For now, let's begin with the bigger picture and consider the core structures that form the basis of defensiveness.

As we try to better understand defense mechanisms and how they work, remember that you might feel defensiveness at just talking about the subject. Sometimes people don't want to admit that they are defensive and can feel uncomfortable exploring the topic. A concept that might be helpful here is *cognitive dissonance*, which refers to holding two contradictory beliefs at the same time (Aronson, 1969). It can also refer to the discomfort that occurs when someone's beliefs and actions don't align with one another (Harmon-Jones & Mills, 2019; Jhangiani & Tarry, 2022). Leon Festinger introduced the concept in 1957, explaining that individuals will actively try to maintain a sense of internal consistency and go to all kinds of lengths to minimize the discomfort they feel at any inconsistencies. For example, perhaps I am a smoker, and yet it is hard to refute the contemporary evidence that smoking is bad for me. But I might do just that, and say that "the research is wrong." I might lash out at someone who reminds me that smoking is unhealthy, saying, "hey, get off my back!" Or, I might stop seeing my doctor who urges me to quit. I might name a counterexample of my aunt who is 92 and has smoked all her life. Often people feel defensive at considering that they might be a "hypocrite" or a "liar" in their own minds.

These are just a few examples of the ways that information can cause discomfort, or even a threat that appears as an "angry bear." Sometimes we can feel fear that leads us to question our own judgments: "Am I wrong? Am I bad? What else am I not seeing?" This might cause shame, embarrassment, sadness, anger, and various reactions to cognitive dissonance. For example, perhaps I consider myself to be an animal lover, and I also eat meat. As a result, I might feel guilty, anxious, and sad.

These examples illustrate just a few of the most common strategies in managing defensiveness, which we might consider as falling into two categories: *externalizing* and *internalizing* tendencies (Gibson, 2015). Externalizing involves placing blame outside oneself when confronted with the threat, such as saying things like, "it's *your* fault!" or "*they* did it!" Those who externalize tend to be reactive, emotionally disruptive, and especially defensive in a more obvious way, such as lashing out and anger. Internalizing involves overly taking responsibility for conflict, attributing the cause of the threat to themselves, saying things like, "it's all *my* fault" and "I'm bad." People who internalize tend to be people-pleasers, often feeling guilt and shame in response to the threat. We all do both of these, depending on the situation. However, some people are more likely to be externalizers, placing blame outside themselves, rather than internalizers, who place all the blame inside themselves (Barber et al., 1994).

Understanding your own tendency to blame others or yourself can help better identify which forms of defensiveness you might use more often. Similarly, understanding the tendency of others to externalize or internalize can help identify which forms they are more likely to use. While theory has its own place and purpose, the intent of this book is to encourage all of us to put ideas into practice. Knowing our habits and when we are prone to externalizing or internalizing can help us recognize and target the areas of work we need to do in order to better respond to our own needs and the reactions of others.

If you are inclined to internalize more often, telling yourself that a conflict or negative emotion is your personal responsibility, then perhaps you might consider how you can share accountability sometimes. You might take a step back to try to see that most interactions are the result of at least two perspectives. If you gravitate toward externalizing, you might learn to ask yourself about the role you played in an interaction that was challenging. How might your words, body language, or tone of voice seem defensive, argumentative, or aggressive? Since we all externalize and internalize, it can also be helpful to know when, in what circumstances, and what specific feelings are connected to your tendencies. For example, perhaps you tend to externalize when you fight with your spouse, but internalize when you have a conflict at work. Or, perhaps you internalize when you are uncomfortable about your parenting, but externalize when you struggle with financial problems. This can help us learn more about how we navigate our emotions and, in particular, how we respond to fear.

It is also important to remember that defense mechanisms can both help and hurt us (Vaillant, 1992). They can allow individuals to temporarily manage stress, emotions, or conflict without causing harm to themselves or others. Sometimes they can also facilitate healthier functioning and emotional regulation. They can be harmful when the very mechanisms are rigid, excessive, or inappropriate, and they prevent individuals from facing reality or growing emotionally. They often hinder mental health, relationships, and overall well-being. It is important to understand a few points about this:

- Everyone engages in defense mechanisms, usually outside of awareness.
- If we can bring our defensive patterns into consciousness, we can heal and grow. Moving them from outside of awareness to a place where

we can observe and witness them creates space for understanding and intentional choices.

- These choices can sometimes mean that we appreciate and value certain forms of protection, while we might seek to change others. We might want to hang on to forms of defensiveness that we have developed over time and that serve us well, while seeking to change or transform other forms of protection that might not help ourselves and others.

THE CHANGE TRIANGLE

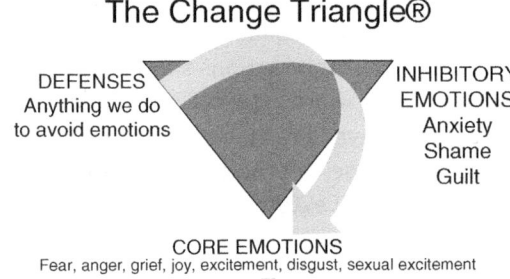

Source: Hilary Jacobs Hendel / https://www.hilaryjacobshendel.com/print-the-change-triangle.

Another way of thinking about why we feel defensive is described by Hendel (2018) in the form of the change triangle. The triangle represents a model for how our defenses work and how we can move to a more calm, less defensive, or "openhearted state." Hendel (2018) explains that *defenses* serve as emotional protection from feeling anything that we do not want to feel, especially pain and feeling overwhelmed. Usually, defenses stop ourselves from feeling *core emotions*, which are inborn, physical sensations, and connected to survival. These include fear, anger, sadness, disgust, joy, excitement, and sexual excitement. We cannot consciously control core emotions as they are hardwired into our brains, and they appear to us as physical sensations.

However, families of origin, culture, and communities have lots of rules about when and how these emotions are allowed, so we learn quickly that they are often not okay. Our brains learn to take action to stop us from feeling the emotions that are not allowed. Because as children it is important to our survival to stay connected to our primary caregivers, we try to avoid punishment. We do this by holding back, suppressing, and restraining ourselves from violating the family and cultural rules. We want to be rewarded, so we stifle and curtail behaviors and expressions that would get us into trouble. This is where *inhibitory emotions* arise, which function to block our core emotions. The word "inhibit" means to keep back, rein in, or hinder. Inhibitory emotions are anxiety, guilt, and shame, and they make us feel connected to our parents and caregivers. As Hendel (2018) explains,

> If my mother leaves the room every time I am distressed, I will eventually learn not to show distress to prevent abandonment. If my anger causes my father to become angry and abusive, I will learn to hide my anger. Inhibitory emotions preserve connection by overriding core emotional expression.
>
> (p. 18)

However, all the work we are doing to prevent ourselves from feeling core emotions also doesn't feel good. We put in a lot of energy to avoid what are hardwired, biological responses to our environment. We have core emotions and inhibitory emotions, all of which we are trying to avoid by using defense mechanisms.

But underneath it all is our *openhearted state*, which Hendel (2018) describes as best understood as the 8 Cs, developed by Richard Schwartz, creator of Internal Family Systems (IFS) therapy (Schwartz, 2023; Schwartz & Sweezy, 2020). The 8 Cs are: calmness, curiosity, clarity, compassion, confidence, courage, creativity, and connectedness. It makes sense then, according to the change triangle, that our defenses are working overtime to protect us from all kinds of negative, unpleasant, overwhelming, and scary emotional experiences. Underneath our defenses live the 8 Cs. If we can bring our defenses to consciousness, we can uncover the 8 Cs.

If we can access our openhearted state (the 8 Cs), we can be aware of our feelings and thoughts as they are happening and avoid knee-jerk, unconscious reactions that can sometimes be destructive to ourselves and others (Hendel, 2018). We can communicate from a grown-up, mature perspective instead of a childlike, immature, automatic place. We can make conscious, thoughtful decisions about how to respond to situations with compassion and curiosity and to try to avoid making an interaction or situation worse. We can use our "wizard" brain and move away from our "lizard" brain. We can take in all the information and have a centered, calm demeanor without further triggering our family, friends, and coworkers.

Both Freud (1923) and Hendel (2018) provide interesting ways to explain the purpose of defensiveness at the individual level, for a single person, inside one's own mind. Another way of exploring the purpose of defensiveness is at a larger, group level. In other words, we might ask questions such as: Who benefits if we are defensive about particular topics, in particular ways?

For example, consider the power of marketing and advertising. Decades of research shows that the main purpose of advertising is to make us feel bad about ourselves (Jhally et al., 2017; Kilbourne, 2000). Ever wonder why so many ads feature beautiful people, or celebrities, often depicting them feeling and looking wonderful? Advertising firms spend lots of money studying various ways that images, colors, words, shapes, and even sounds, can make us feel insecure and shameful (Lindstrom, 2011). They do this in order to create feelings of jealousy and envy in us, their audience, because they know this works to get us to buy their products. In other words, the systems of marketing and advertising want to make us feel a certain way in order to serve their commercial interests. This functions as a tool of consumerism and capitalism. These systems (marketing, advertising, consumerism, and capitalism) are designed to make us feel bad as individuals and as groups. It is not that there is one specific person in charge of all of these systems, which have been operating for centuries now. However, it is in the best interest of these social structures and institutions to work in this way.

We might continue to ask: What is the cost of defensiveness for both *individuals* and *groups*? Who and what is served by our defensiveness? Usually, the answer to these questions requires us to look at systems of power. It is often the people in charge of institutions that want to make sure they stay at the top. We can define *institutions* as structures of social order that govern the behavior of groups, and, in this case, we will think about them as formal organizations such as the church, government, hospitals, prisons, schools, and the like (Caporaso & Jupille, 2022; Knight, 1992; North, 1991). We might think of society as a pyramid, with stratified layers. Those in power are at the top (they are the fewest) and those with less power are at the bottom (there are more of them). The people at the top are those with the most power, the ones who control the institutions, and they make rules and laws that protect people like them. Imagine the people who run the government, own Fortune 500 companies, own hospital conglomerates, or major corporations. Think about the individuals who have been: the

Pope, presidents, or billionaires. Overall, these people tend to be white, male or masculine, middle-upper class, heterosexual, Christian, educated, and able-bodied, especially in the United States.

It is important to note that this discussion of power and privilege is not about pointing fingers at individuals. In even the harshest regimes around the world, one individual cannot control an entire society. You might notice that you may already be feeling defensive while reading this, as if there is a suggestion that all white men are to blame for all wrongdoings, or that each individual white man is a problem. That is not the point. Instead, we are stepping back, looking at how large systems function, and noticing that in general, U.S. culture has laws and policies that benefit some while marginalizing others, giving some people opportunities that everyone is not afforded. You might note how you are feeling about this information as we will delve deeper into understanding it later.

Now let's return to the change triangle (Hendel, 2018). If we live in a culture that dictates that men should never show "weakness" and that "strength" is defined by expressing anger, then when men (and masculinized people) do feel normal human emotions (such as sadness), then they will create all kinds of defenses to prevent themselves from feeling it. The culture tends to punish men for crying, expressing grief or any emotion that makes that person appear vulnerable. We say things like, "Be a man! Suck it up!" and teach boys from an early age that it is not appropriate to violate this important social rule. Similarly, we tell women and girls that they should not feel or express anger. So, when they do inevitably have this very human experience of rage, we punish them, telling them to "Act like a lady! Don't be crazy! Calm down!" The rules of the culture make sure that feminized and masculinized people "stay in their places" and do not violate social norms related to gender (Lips, 2018). The social structure as a whole benefits from these strict gender rules for all kinds of reasons. There is not one individual in charge of these norms; in fact, in the United States, for example, we were all born into a society where we learned these rules. But rules about gender have changed over time and across cultures (Lips, 2018) which is how we can trace the ways that societies have benefited from different expectations in different spaces throughout history.

To summarize, not only should we question how defensiveness works in our individual psychologies, but also explore its purpose at a cultural level, too. This reminds us that our lives are situated not just in our own personal histories of our families, neighborhoods, and traditions, but in a broader context of institutional structures, like education, healthcare, religion, and government (House, 1981).

COPING VS. DEFENSIVENESS

It may be important to notice here that *defensiveness* can sound a lot like *coping*. While there may be some similarities between them, psychologists tend to see them as two separate phenomena. Both coping and defenses can share a common purpose in managing our negative feelings such as stress and anxiety (Cramer, 1998). However, they differ in that coping is a more conscious, intentional process (Affleck & Tennen, 1996) while defense mechanisms are more unconscious and unintentional.

Defense mechanisms are "under water," to use the metaphor of the iceberg, whereas coping strategies are mostly "above water," where we can see them. Lazarus and Folkman (1984) distinguished between different types of coping with two categories. The first is problem-focused coping, which involves "doing something" externally to solve a problem. For example, if I have a flat tire, I may go to a mechanic to have it repaired. If I have a paper to write or a presentation to give for my job, I might use time management skills to work backward, preparing small tasks toward the due date. The focus of attention is addressed on the problem itself.

The second category is emotion-focused coping (Lazarus & Folkman, 1984), where one "does something" to "feel better." For instance, if I have a fight with my spouse, I might write down my emotions to try to get them out of my head before having a conversation later. If I have a bad day at work, I might eat a bowl of ice cream. While these are examples of a more healthy and less healthy choice, the focus of attention is on the emotion experienced. Generally speaking, it is the active and purposeful "doing" that differentiates coping from defensiveness, although there is a great deal of overlap.

Exercise

In your own words, answer the following questions:

1. What is defensiveness?
2. Why is defensiveness considered unconscious?
3. Name one takeaway message you learned from Part 1.
4. Name one question or wondering you are left with after reading Part 1.

Exercise

Scenario

Emily and Danielle are coworkers who've been assigned to work together on a project. They've had some tension in the past, but they're trying to make it work. Today, they're discussing how to approach a particular part of the project.

DANIELLE: *(leaning over the desk, looking at Emily's work)*
Emily, I noticed that the report you submitted still has a lot of the same issues we talked about last time. There are some major mistakes, and the information is not consistent. We really need to fix that before the meeting tomorrow.

EMILY: *(immediately crossing her arms and leaning back in her chair)*
Well, I'm doing the best I can. You know, not everyone has the same attention to detail as you do. Maybe you could just trust that I'm handling it? I don't need constant micromanagement.

DANIELLE: *(raising her eyebrows, feeling irritated)*
I'm just trying to help. This is important, and if we don't address these problems now, it's going to reflect poorly on both of us. I'm not trying to micromanage you, just pointing out things that need to be corrected.

EMILY: *(defensive, rolling her eyes)*
Well, maybe if you actually helped instead of pointing out problems all the time, we wouldn't be in this situation. You're always so quick to criticize. It's not helpful.

DANIELLE: *(frowning, a bit frustrated)*
I'm not criticizing you. I'm just saying we need to get it right. Can we focus on the solution here instead of getting defensive?

EMILY: *(looking away, her voice sharp)*
If you want to "focus on the solution," maybe you could start by taking some responsibility for your part of the project, too. You're not perfect either, you know.

Questions About the Scenario

1. Do you think Emily is using more externalizing or internalizing defenses? Why?
2. Do you think Danielle is using more externalizing or internalizing defenses? Why?
3. Why do you think defensiveness is so common in workplace conversations, especially when there's pressure or a feeling of being judged?

4. From your own experience, what strategies could Emily and Danielle use to move from defensiveness toward a more collaborative and solution-focused conversation? How can they both take accountability without feeling attacked?

SUMMARY

Part 1 introduced and defined defensiveness. We reviewed some reasons why you should read this book and some learning outcomes. Part 1 offered some theories and concepts to consider in our forthcoming discussion, including the iceberg, the bear, lizard vs. wizard brain, emotional intelligence, and emotional granularity. We explored the purpose of defensiveness, considering cognitive dissonance, externalizing and internalizing tendencies, and the change triangle. We examined how individuals and systems have a stake in defensiveness and how it can function for both people and organizations. Lastly, we distinguished between coping and defensiveness.

Now let's turn our attention to why we sometimes feel defensive, so that we can better understand how to identify and recognize how it appears in ourselves and others.

Chapter 2
Why Do We Sometimes Feel Defensive?

On Thursday, the class discusses case studies from the assigned reading. One story features a white student who shuts down during a group discussion on race, insisting they "didn't own slaves" and shouldn't be made to feel guilty. The students are asked to reflect on their reactions.

The conversation grows heated.

A student named Carter—one of the athletes from the back—leans forward.

"I'm not trying to start anything," he begins, "but sometimes it does feel like white people get treated like villains in these conversations. Like, some of us are just trying to learn, but it's like walking on eggshells."

A couple of students nod. A few shift in their seats.

Tasha, a soft-spoken student near the window, raises her hand. Her voice is quiet but firm.

Transforming Defensiveness: A Guidebook for Rewriting Our Stories & Reclaiming Connection, First Edition. Andrea L. Dottolo.
© 2026 John Wiley & Sons, Inc. All rights reserved, including rights for text and data mining and training of artificial intelligence technologies or similar technologies. Published 2026 by John Wiley & Sons, Inc.

"But that discomfort is part of the learning. I'm not saying anyone should feel guilty for being white. But we've had to carry these conversations for generations. And now, finally, it's being discussed in classrooms. So yeah, it's gonna be uncomfortable. It's been uncomfortable for us forever."

The room is silent for a beat.

Dr. Felix breaks it gently. "Both of you are naming important truths," she says. "Feeling accused is not the same as being attacked. But feeling invisible, unheard, or erased—that's also real. Our job is to sit with that tension. To listen, without trying to escape it."

She writes on the board:

Discomfort is not danger. Silence is not neutrality. Curiosity is not weakness.

During the last ten minutes of class, she opens the floor to anonymous questions submitted on index cards. She reads a few aloud:

- "How do I stop being defensive when someone challenges me? I don't even notice until later."
- "I grew up in a conservative family. How do I have these conversations at home without being shut down—or shutting them down?"
- "What if I'm part of a marginalized group and someone says I have privilege? It feels confusing."
- "Why does it feel like only certain identities are allowed to be talked about in class?"
- "I've been told I'm too emotional when I talk about this stuff. Is that a bad thing?"

Dr. Felix reads each question with care, thanking the students for their honesty. She doesn't try to answer all of them today. Instead, she posts them to the class forum and promises they'll return to them—again and again.

In the coming weeks, the students will dig deeper into theories of oppression, implicit bias, and emotional regulation. Some will push back. Some will have breakthroughs. And some will, quietly, begin to change—not just their minds, but their hearts.

This chapter explores some of the underlying reasons for defensiveness. It may be helpful for us to understand the "why" behind feeling defensive, or the fuel that can inform some of the ways that defensiveness can show up. There are many reasons why anyone might feel defensive, but identifying some of the primary or root causes can help us examine what motivates our reactions and behaviors. Self-knowledge can foster emotional self-regulation and positively contribute to the quality of our interpersonal relationships (Asadi et al., 2022). The "why" can inform many, if not all, of the different ways that we experience and witness defensiveness in our lives.

Let's explore some of the underlying reasons or manifestations of *why* we feel defensive (Dottolo, 2019). This list is not exhaustive, and simply introduces a few forms. You will notice that they sometimes overlap and inform each other. I offer examples and exercises to illustrate them, while remembering that we all experience many different kinds of threats (or bears). Along the way, you might consider some other reasons why people might feel defensive. As you move through the examples and exercises, try to think of instances from your own experiences. Try to notice which ones are easier for you to notice and identify and which ones are more difficult. Sometimes the hardest and most challenging reflections can teach us the most. If you are earnest in your exploration and bring curiosity to the conversation, you may be surprised at how useful your new tools can be.

IN-GROUP BIAS

In general, bias refers to an inclination or tendency toward or against a person, thing, or idea, usually in a way that is disproportionate, unfair, or inaccurate (Cambridge Dictionary, 2017; Steinbock, 1978). *In-group bias* involves favoring one's own group, based on identification (Tajfel & Turner, 1979). We tend to defend our "in-group" while opposing those who are not a member of the group (Molenberghs, 2013). Simply assigning people to temporary groups can trigger in-group bias, such as in team sports and group projects. When discussing issues we feel strongly about, in-group bias can be especially apparent. We can become attached to a position which we consider the "right" way to do things according to our cultural norms and practices. Those not part of the in-group are seen as outsiders, peculiar, not "like me," often "less than" or not relevant (Brewer, 1979).

For example, people tend to feel strongly about child rearing, especially beliefs about sleeping. North American parents have tended to expect their babies to sleep alone. They have bassinets, cribs, strollers, and other ways that they encourage infants to sleep alone. Sometimes they even sleep in a separate room, like a nursery. North American culture has tended to foster the belief that this encourages independence and fits with a sense of individualism that is a part of the culture. In many other cultures, infants sleep with their mother for their first few years of life (Keller et al., 2005). One reason for this, among many others, is that they need to be close to their infant throughout the night, in case the baby is hungry, scared, or in danger. Sometimes people have responded to this information with in-group bias, suggesting that the North American way is "normal" or universal and the others are "weird," as they might say, and perhaps even detrimental. They might think, "Those people don't love their children. It's not healthy to have a baby that doesn't know how to self-soothe. The kid can't sleep with their mother forever!" Meanwhile, members of the group that sleep with their infant might think, "Those people don't love their children. It's not healthy to leave a baby all alone. That is child abuse!" This example illustrates how strong in-group bias can be and how it functions to protect us from information we might find threatening. If members of one group consider that others sleep with their babies differently, they then worry that their own practices might not be the "only" way, or worse, that they might be harming their child. This is threatening information, so our brains find ways to protect us from what we perceive to be a threat. In this case, protecting our own strong beliefs about sleep routines for children. This example also demonstrates that sometimes there is not a "right" or a "wrong" way, but simply different ways.

This defense is easy to see as connected to the change triangle (Hendel, 2018), an unconscious way of keeping us connected to our "tribe." We cling to our past, our history, our feelings of belonging, and can feel threatened by other ways of being and behaving in the world.

This can be connected to our core sense of self, our identity, how we understand ourselves in relation to others (Yap & Ichikawa, 2024). This example is also related to the ways that culture and systems are invested in influencing the ways that we feel about what we think is "natural" or "normal."

Exercise: I Am

Fill in the following blanks with words that describe you. If I were to ask you, "Who are you?" and you could not use your name as an answer, what other words would you use to identify yourself? You might consider some labels that define you. You might consider groups in which you are a member. These could be broad, large identities or categories and/or smaller identities or groups.

I am _____ _____ (number)

I am _____ _____

I am _____ _____

I am _____ _____

I am _____ _____

Now rate how strongly you identify each of these groups on a scale of 1–5, where 1 = do not identify at all to 5 = strongly identify. Use the spaces next to the descriptions you chose. In other words, think about how much each of these words describe who you are. You might indicate a number next to each word that you wrote.

1	2	3	4	5
Very little	a little	neither a little nor a lot	a lot	very much

For those identities that you rated higher (4 or 5), this indicates that you feel strongly about these identities and that they are likely an important part of how you see yourself. For each of the labels you chose, consider that they are all group identities, meaning that you learned them in the context of other people with those same characteristics. For example, if I said, "I am a woman," I learned early on in my life that there exists a group, a category, called "woman" or "girl" and I was informed that I am a member of that group. This is true even for labels that seem like individual personality traits. For instance, if I stated, "I am shy," I still had to learn somewhere that there are other people that are also shy and that descriptor applies to me.

For the identities or descriptors that I feel strongly about (I rated as 4 or 5), then in-group bias might be easily triggered for me. If I feel very strongly about being a woman and when someone says something negative about women, or makes a generalization about all women, I might respond with defensiveness.

Once I was teaching about white racial identity, and a young, traditional aged college student who was also a white man became aggressive in response to learning about the material. He stood up, red-faced, and charged me, as though he would hit me, yelling, "You can't say that! That's not true! White people don't have privilege!" This student was very strongly identified as a white man and perceived the scholarship about the topic to threaten his *in-group bias*. After trying to de-escalate the situation for some time, it became clear that he was also a danger to other students, whereupon I had to dismiss the class and call campus police.

In contrast, for those identities that I do not feel particularly strongly about (rated 1–3), I may or may not feel in-group bias. For example, if I stated that "I am a New Yorker" but I do not feel particularly tied to that identifier, if someone says something negative about New York, I might not care.

An important component to in-group bias is that we tend to oppose and even demonize the "others" (Buttelmann & Bohm, 2014). We can take the position that we are superior, or "correct" in our way of thinking according to the practices of our group. Often, the characteristics of the group are generalized to all members, but not beyond the group. Furthermore, the out-group, or the "others," are also made to appear as if "they" are all the same. This is the foundation of "us/them" thinking. For example, if I stated, "I am an American," I might believe that there are essential qualities that all Americans have, perhaps including beliefs, morals, and values. If I feel threatened as an American, as in the case of 9/11 when the Twin Towers in New York City and the Pentagon were attacked by foreign terrorists, my ideas about being an American might get even stronger, and, in doing so, my feelings about out-groups are also heightened, as we see in the motto shared by some at the time, "If you are not with us, then you are against us."

If we step back and look at the bigger picture of institutions and social structures, it is understandable why those in power would promote this way of thinking. This kind of defensiveness can serve as propaganda, uniting nationalist ideologies, used to justify all kinds of actions, including war. This can be a kind of strategic psychology, used by many politicians and leaders all over the world. We also know that wars take place for many reasons, often centered on the interests of people in power, including making money. A good example of this practice is represented in the film *Wag the Dog*, where a Hollywood director and public relations specialist make up a fake war as a way to cover up a high-profile sex scandal—and it worked (Levinson, 1997). In-group bias can serve to protect not only our individual psyches but also collective identity and political priorities.

In-group bias shares similarities with another cognitive bias called *confirmation bias*, which is "the tendency for people to seek out and favor information that confirms their expectations and beliefs" (Jhangiani & Tarry, 2022). Confirmation bias is often unnoticed but is a strong influence in reinforcing in-group bias, especially as it appears in digital technology and social media (Modgil et al., 2024). Sometimes internet algorithms infiltrate the information received by an individual. The internet keeps track of the type of ads we select and which news stories we choose to read (Ling, 2020). Over continued tracking, the algorithm can be constructed to profile our personal choices and political views (Modgil et al., 2024). This profile influences the information we are exposed to, and the internet will feed us the particular news or information that will reinforce our views, often while we are totally unaware of this bias. This aids in confirming to us that our bias against a group, ideology, or institution is valid based on being exposed to information that continues to agree and support our strongly held beliefs (Cornell, 2024). Our phones and other electronic devices can hear us speaking and keep track of the kinds of things we say, so that ads and information that match our speech automatically appear on our feeds (Norton.com).

These ideas can develop into such a strong bias that even when evidence and facts are presented that refute these beliefs, we can still hold firmly onto our position (Sumeracki & Kaminske, 2024). Sometimes contradicting evidence goes ignored, or is considered irrelevant (Rassin, 2008). For example, when someone believes a conspiracy theory, they only read sources that confirm their ideas while disregarding more validated or reliable evidence. Some people believe that vaccines cause autism and then only consult information and individual stories that say that very thing (Foster & Ortiz, 2017). At the same time, they pay no attention to the many scientific studies that say otherwise. Sometimes they even actively attack the research, accusing the many researchers of bias themselves.

INTERSECTIONALITY

Since in-group bias is based on our identities, it is important to keep in mind another important concept about identities which is called *intersectionality*. We must be cautious not to isolate any one identity, or approach it as if it might exist as separated, context-free, and/or uninfluenced by other parts of ourselves. For example, if I identify as white, it is important to emphasize that my race does not exist in isolation, somehow separate from my gender, class, age, sexuality, and other identities. Intersectionality is the idea that individuals exist at the *intersection* of many identities and social realities, all informed and shaped by the others (Crenshaw et al., 1995; Dottolo & Stewart, 2008; King, 1997; Spelman, 1988). Patricia Hill Collins (1990) described intersectionality as an "interlocking matrix of relationships" (p. 20). The isolation of race as a singular category can result in ignoring other identities and experiences based on other parts of our selves.

For example, while it can be interesting to consider white people as a group, that group will have lots of in-group variation, such as experiences connected to gender and class. Furthermore, let's say we are interested in a study of upper-class white people (Ostrander, 1984).

While wealthy, white men and women might have a lot in common, it would be inaccurate to claim that their social identities are the *same*. Similarly, white upper-class women and white working-class women may or may not share similar experiences of whiteness, but certainly have differing access to opportunities, economic advantage, and institutional power.

In a retrospective study of high school experiences, Ortner (2003) found that race, class, and gender all mattered in the lives of her participants then and now. Her ethnographic study *New Jersey Dreaming: Capital, Culture, and the Class of '58* (2003) provides a rich account of the lives of working- and middle-class students from a New Jersey high school, focusing on how their experiences evolved over time. Ortner's primary concern is the impact of social class—both the class origins of her subjects and how class position was maintained or changed over time. She shows that the postwar American dream of upward mobility was more accessible for some than others, depending on their multiple identities. Gender shaped educational and occupational opportunities. Women in the class of '58 faced limited expectations around careers and were often pushed toward marriage and domesticity. Those who pursued work often ended up in feminized, lower-paying professions (e.g., secretarial work), highlighting how *gender and class* intersected to restrict women's opportunities. Middle-class students had better tools (cultural, educational, and social) for adapting to economic changes, while working-class students often struggled. Again, their experiences matter not necessarily only as the result of individual social identities, but in the ways in which they intersect.

Another example involves research about Black women's attitudes about the women's movement. Some authors have discussed the pressured position of Black women in having to "choose" between race and gender loyalties, with divided alliances between political causes and social identities (Giddings, 1984; bell hooks, 1989; King, 1975). An intersectional perspective highlights that Black women are not *either* Black *or* women and often support *both* the Civil Rights *and* women's movements (Cole & Stewart, 1996; Gay & Tate, 1998; Hunter & Sellers, 1998).

From a psychological perspective, people who occupy marginalized identities often develop complex defense mechanisms in response to chronic systemic stressors, such as racism, sexism, and homophobia. These are not simply internal, individual issues, but deeply tied to external environments and repeated experiences of invalidation, threat, or discrimination (Comas-Díaz et al., 2019).

Intersectionality is related to defensiveness because it encourages us to consider our identities as they intersect with cultural, social, and systemic pressures. It allows us to view defenses as meaningful survival strategies. This lens also pushes us to consider how defensiveness is a response to oppression (Wing Sue et al., 2009). Defense mechanisms are not just internal; they are often reflections of the social world. Intersectionality allows us to see how structures of power shape the emotional lives of individuals and how defenses can function as both shields and signals of deeper psychological and social dynamics.

Exercise

Choose one of the identities you named in the previous exercise to which you feel strongly connected (you rated 4–5). It may even be the identity you listed first in the list. Think about an instance in which you felt you needed to defend that identity. For example, perhaps someone said something insulting or offensive about the group to which you belong. You can write your ideas here:

- What happened? What was said? Who said it?
- How did the comment or incident affect your feelings about your own group?
- What did you feel? (try to use emotion words, such as happy, sad, and/or angry)
- How did it affect your feelings about the out-group(s)? What did you feel? (try to use emotion words, such as happy, sad, and/or angry)

Exercise: The Neighborhood Game—Identifying In-Group Bias

Scenario:
Imagine you're part of a community project team tasked with organizing an annual neighborhood festival. The group consists of members from two different sections of the neighborhood: *Eastview* and *Westbrook*. Each section has its own distinct characteristics, such as cultural traditions, economic

background, and local sports teams. The Eastview section tends to be more affluent, while Westbrook is a working-class area. As you start planning, different ideas are brought up, and people from each section suggest ways to represent their community at the festival.

Eastview Team Member's Idea:
"We should have a VIP tent with catered food, exclusive seating, and an open bar for the 'important' guests. Our community loves these luxury experiences, and it'll make our section shine in front of others."

Westbrook Team Member's Idea:
"How about we have a booth with homemade food, featuring dishes from our own neighborhood's families? We could showcase our community's hard work and creativity through food. Plus, it'll bring a more authentic vibe to the event."

Questions

1. What are the assumptions about each section's values, needs, or preferences that might be based on stereotypes or in-group loyalty?
2. How did you feel when the Eastview team member suggested a VIP experience for an 'elite' group of people? Did this feel fair to everyone? Why or why not?
3. When considering the Westbrook idea, what assumptions might someone from Eastview have about it? Would these assumptions be based on in-group bias?
4. Do you think one section's idea is "better" than the other? Why might this happen, and how could in-group bias influence this opinion?
5. Can you think of real-life examples where people have treated others differently based on their group (such as neighborhood, social class, or background)? How might in-group bias show up in those situations?

STEREOTYPES & DISCRIMINATION

This discussion of bias is deeply related to another concept you might be familiar with—*stereotypes*, which are the "positive or negative beliefs that we hold about the characteristics of a social group" (Jhangiani & Tarry, 2022, p. 743). Our in-group bias is an example of the positive beliefs we hold toward the members of the groups to which we belong. In contrast, we can sometimes form negative beliefs about groups to which we do not belong, often referred to as *prejudice* (Jhangiani & Tarry, 2022). If you look closely at the word prejudice, it is made up of the prefix "pre" meaning "to come before" and the root of the word, meaning "to judge." Therefore, prejudice is simply a way that we judge people before we know them, simply because they belong to a group, "prejudging" them. This can be for any reason. I might decide I don't like tall people because they can reach things that I cannot, and that makes me angry. I think they are arrogant. In this instance, I have a *prejudice* toward tall people. Prejudice exists only in my head, reflected in my thoughts and beliefs about these tall individuals.

Discrimination is another related concept that sometimes is confused with prejudice. Discrimination is the differential treatment of someone based on their group membership (Moreau, 2010). This means that someone takes action based on their prejudice. If I give failing grades to all of the tall students in my class, regardless of their academic performance, this is discrimination. Typically discrimination applies to members of marginalized groups, often around issues of gender, race, class, sexuality, age, nationality, body size, disability, and so forth (https://www.apa.org/topics/racism-bias-discrimination). For example, when people of color search for apartments, and landlords suddenly say that the apartments are no longer vacant or rents become outrageously high (Yamato, 1990).

While prejudices and biases might create a false sense of safety, they can also be harmful to our personal relationships and workplace interactions (https://www.psychologytoday.com/us/basics/bias). We often act in discriminatory ways toward people who are not like us. These unconscious, knee-jerk reactions based on stereotypical beliefs are often the result of learned attitudes. People are highly influenced by their family background, race, social class, education, religious institutions, and, certainly, media exposure that may depict marginalized groups with negative traits and characteristics. Consider the history of sports teams using Native Americans as their mascots in dehumanizing, cartoon characters and the ways that affects how we think and feel about Native people (Roppolo, 2013, https://www.apa.org/pi/oema/resources/indian-mascots).

Stereotyping is a kind of social categorization of an entire group, which is one of the reasons for prejudice (McLeod, 2023—https://www.simplypsychology.org/katz-braly.html). The term "ageism" was introduced in 1969 by Robert Butler. He describes it as "a form of bigotry we tend to overlook," where young and middle-aged people can feel uncomfortable toward older folks. Studies indicate that over time, age stereotypes have become more negative (Levy, 2017; Mason et al., 2015). For example, older women are rendered invisible in the culture, exemplified in films, where 80% of characters over the age of 50 are men (Geena Davis Institute, https://geenadavisinstitute. org/research/women-over-50-the-right-to-be-seen-on-screen/#:~:text= Characters%20aged%2050%2B%20constitute%20less,and%2066%25% 20in%20streaming%20platforms, 2024). Other studies show that employers frequently believe that older workers are "less productive and less comfortable with technology" (Börsch-Supan, 2013; DeNisco, 2016). Applewhite (2019) explains that ageism is a social concept, illustrated in the fact that in other cultures and past societies, people who survived into old age were rare and respected. Contemporary beauty standards tell us that young is beautiful, and so we ignore older people, making them nearly invisible in the media (Kilbourne, 2000). We endorse stereotypes that describe older people as a "drain on society," with declining abilities to contribute to society (Applewhite, 2019). We tend to believe that they are less capable, incompetent, and "out of touch," and no longer economically useful.

These examples illustrate how people in power benefit from marginalizing older people. We learn to feel this way from the culture (prejudice) and sometimes take actions to disregard, ignore, or mistreat older people (discrimination). "Like all discrimination, [ageism] legitimizes and sustains inequalities between groups, in this case, between the young and the no longer young" (Applewhite, 2019, p. 9).

If we think back to the iceberg, ageism is an example of a stereotyping that often goes unnoticed, outside our awareness. It is also an example of an identity that changes over time. In other words, as we grow and develop, we might think about "those" old people as weak, frail, and dependent (Applewhite, 2019). However, if we are lucky enough to age ourselves, then quite quickly "we" become those old people, navigating these negative stereotypes against "us." In other words, what was once "those" people may eventually become "us."

Prejudice, stereotyping and discrimination are easy to see when discussing in-group bias. However, it is important to note that these concepts not only influence one another, but can be underlying causes for many forms of defensiveness.

Exercise

While our environment can lead us to be attracted to personal likes and dislikes, we are often not aware of our biases. This is related to our earlier point about defensiveness in that many of our attitudes and feelings exist outside of our awareness, in our unconscious.

An important line of research on this very topic began in 1998 about implicit bias, where researchers are still collecting data on this large project. Try as many of the different tests as you like at their website here:

https://implicit.harvard.edu/implicit/takeatest.html

Pause and Reflect:
- What was it like to take the test?
- What attitudes or beliefs did you have about yourself and/or your target groups (the people the test was about) before you began the test?
- Were you surprised at your results?
- Did you notice any defensiveness coming up for you while taking the test? After receiving your results?

It is critical when confronting stereotyping bias that awareness of these prejudices be heightened and recognized. A purposeful, conscious recognition, and deliberate self-awareness of personal bias can lead to reduced discrimination and greater open-heartedness (Hendel, 2018). Judgments made from a reflective perspective, critically examining conscious and unconscious stereotyping and paying attention to beliefs based on a lifetime of learned bias can produce better understanding of oneself and the culture in which we live.

BELIEF IN A JUST WORLD

Belief in a just world is the faith, trust, and confidence that the world is fair, where "just" is derived from the word "justice" (Lerner, 1965). In other words, the belief that "good things tend to happen to good people, and bad things happen to bad people" (Furnham, 2003).

Exercise

Rate each statement according to your personal beliefs.

1. If I work hard, I can succeed.

1	2	3	4	5
strongly disagree	disagree	neither agree nor disagree	agree	strongly agree

2. People who do not succeed are just plain lazy.

1	2	3	4	5
strongly disagree	disagree	neither agree nor disagree	agree	strongly agree

3. Failure is almost always the fault of the individual.

1	2	3	4	5
strongly disagree	disagree	neither agree nor disagree	agree	strongly agree

4. We have plenty of aid and relief programs to provide for everyone if people would just make use of them.

1	2	3	4	5
strongly disagree	disagree	neither agree nor disagree	agree	strongly agree

5. Addiction is just a lack of willpower.

1	2	3	4	5
strongly disagree	disagree	neither agree nor disagree	agree	strongly agree

What is your total score, if you add all your responses together?_____

If your total score was between 15 and 25, then you tend to believe in a just world. If your total was lower than 15 (with 5 being the lowest), then you are less influenced by this ideology.

The belief in a just world is a deeply held American idea, and it has many different labels. You may have encountered this before with the label "the American Dream" (Samuel, 2012). This is the idea that if I work hard and I do good things, I will be rewarded. This idea is also known as "the just world hypothesis," which refers to the prediction that the world is fair and just (Goodman & Carr, 2017; Lerner & Miller, 1978). You may have also seen it referred to as "the myth of the meritocracy" (Liu, 2011). The word "meritocracy" is composed of two parts—the first part, "merit," means worth or accomplishment, and the second part, "-ocracy," refers to a system of rule, like democracy. So, a meritocracy is a system of rule based on an individual's efforts and accomplishments.

The tendency to believe that one's lot in life is solely the responsibility of the individual is a deeply ingrained defense mechanism to help us have faith in a just world. For example, I was on the job market for many years after I earned my PhD, applying for hundreds of jobs in those years. Sometimes I was offered an interview, but I never landed the position that I wanted. I do not want to believe that the reason I was overlooked had anything to do with my gender, ethnicity, culture, sexuality, or social class. I want to believe that someone else was simply more qualified for the job. Perhaps they had more teaching experience, or published more than I did, or were a better "fit" for the position. I want to believe it was because I did not deserve the job, and that there was another candidate better qualified than I. I do not want to believe that I was rejected for any other reason that would seem "unfair." This would cause fear, anxiety, and shake our much needed faith in fairness and a just system. Encountering information that does not seem "fair" can evoke defensiveness.

A central component of the belief in a just world is that if I believe that I work hard, then I will succeed, then I also *must* believe that "those people," the ones who are not as successful as I am, are not successful because they are lazy, stupid, and did not work hard enough (Dottolo, 2019). According to belief in a just world, "those people" who are not as fortunate as I am deserve this mistreatment, injustice, or marginalized conditions in which they live. Unfortunately, we all know people who work really hard and cannot seem to pay their bills or accomplish what they wish. This part of the myth of the meritocracy is called *downward social comparison* by social psychologists (Gibbons & Gerrard, 1989; Jhangiani & Tarry, 2022; Tiggemann & Policy, 2010). This involves evaluating people who are worse off than us in order to make ourselves feel better, to create a positive image of ourselves. If we subscribe to the idea that we are where we are because of merit and hard work, then downward social comparison is necessary to sustain this ideology.

Furthermore, the belief in a just world also includes the idea that "those people" who are more successful than I am, who have more than I do, are there because they worked harder than I did, they deserve it, and they must be better and smarter than I am. Again, we all know about people who did nothing and have everything. Not surprisingly, social psychologists call this *upward social comparison* (Collins, 1996; van de Ven, 2017), where we explain that people who are better off than us are more valuable or work harder than we do. Such comparison can make us feel bad about ourselves and also creates envy and competition (Muller & Fayant, 2010; van de Ven, 2017).

This part of the myth of the meritocracy serves power structures (like capitalism) by ensuring that individuals stay competitive with each other and internalize their failures. Both of these outcomes protect those in power from having to be accountable or responsible for their behaviors or their position in the hierarchy. Social comparison, both downward and upward personal comparisons with others, can be used as a strategy to help us more clearly understand our status and provide us with information to determine how we are doing (Nortje, 2020). It is normal to assess how our abilities and achievements compare with others we look up to or consider lesser than ourselves. However, negative consequences can become evident when we exclude individuals based on these comparisons, or when feelings of inadequacy and inferiority develop.

Upward social comparisons can result in excluding those we feel are far superior and extremely different from us. We may feel they cannot be considered part of our social group because they are so very different from us. The superior intelligence of Einstein may have intimidated others. The supermodel who is deemed the perfect physical example of beauty may be shunned by those who feel unable to compete with her slenderness and beauty. These feelings of inferiority and jealousy can result in bitterness, depression, and potential isolation (Festinger, 1954; Tesser, 1988).

Another interesting feature about all of these phrases (belief in a just world, American Dream, just world hypothesis, and the myth of the meritocracy) is that the wording may be different, but the message is the same, conveying lack of clarity and truth. Notice that it is "a *belief* in a just world," not a fact. We call it "the just world *hypothesis*" which is not a conclusion or a result. It is "the *myth* of the meritocracy," which is a story, or a widely held false belief. And lastly, we call it "the American *Dream*," not a reality or truth. Embedded in the language we use to refer to this precious and treasured American ideas is the recognition that it is a fantasy, or at minimum, very doubtful.

Exercise

To explore the belief in the just world, consider the following practices and policies and respond according to how much you agree or disagree with them. Indicate the degree to which you agree with these statements or facts.

1. Children of alumni receive preference for admission into some private colleges.

1	2	3	4	5
strongly disagree	disagree	neither agree nor disagree	agree	strongly agree

2. Persons accused of a crime who cannot post bail are imprisoned and thus appear in court dressed in prison uniform, often in handcuffs.

1	2	3	4	5
strongly disagree	disagree	neither agree nor disagree	agree	strongly agree

3. An employment agency advertises for an "All-American type" to fill a public relations position.

1	2	3	4	5
strongly disagree	disagree	neither agree nor disagree	agree	strongly agree

4. Employees of a particular university are allowed free tuition, as are their spouses.

1	2	3	4	5
strongly disagree	disagree	neither agree nor disagree	agree	strongly agree

5. A corporation decides to fill an opening "in-house" rather than advertise.

1	2	3	4	5
strongly disagree	disagree	neither agree nor disagree	agree	strongly agree

(The previous items are from: https://www.apa.org/pi/ses/resources/publications/institutional-discrimination-obrien.pdf)

Are your scores from these five questions similar or different from the five questions at the beginning of this section? The same scale from the previous section applies to these questions too. That is, higher scores indicate more endorsement of a belief in a just world.

INVESTMENT IN THE STATUS QUO

Investment in the status quo, also called status quo bias, is the idea that we are attached to the way things are now—we care deeply about a system that rewards certain characteristics and behaviors (Silver & Mitchell, 1990). The desire to keep things "the way they are" is a form of protection against any discomfort, suffering, or loss of power as a result of any changes in the system (Dottolo, 2019; Fleming et al., 2010).

For example, let's say I love to drink from plastic straws. Every time I go to a restaurant I ask for a straw. I like that it makes my drink feel "special." It's easy to drink, and I don't have to put my mouth on a potentially dirty glass. It reminds me of being a kid, or drinking something fun, like a milkshake. Recently we have learned that plastic straws are very damaging to the environment, and many restaurants now have policies that do not use them anymore (Roy et al., 2021; Viera et al., 2020). Some have switched to paper straws, but some simply do not carry straws at all. So when I go to a restaurant, I might be mad, or sad, or frustrated that I don't "get" to have my straw. These reactions are protecting me from the disappointment and discomfort that result from the change in the status quo. This example centers on a mundane and somewhat trivial way that we are "invested" in ideas and behaviors, and therefore may be potentially threatened if they change.

Some families are "invested" in a political party. Perhaps your North American family has been Republican for generations. Your brothers, father, uncles, and grandfathers all fought in a war, whether it was Iraq, Afghanistan, Somalia, Vietnam, Korea, World War II, and the like. Your sisters, mother, aunts, and grandmothers were all "patriotic" supporters of the military and always voted Republican. So when someone asks you about your political affiliation, you say "Republican," but not necessarily because you value the beliefs, practices, and platform of the Republican party, but because that's what you're "supposed" to be. You even think that the current Republican party looks very different than it once did and has changed in important ways, but you just stay Republican because you are invested in a system, a military, or a family that just always was.

Another example is from a sensational tabloid headline that is printed periodically. It always says, "Who's gay? Who's not?" and the cover displays photos of suspected gay and lesbian celebrities, always including one that might be "surprising" to learn that they were not heterosexual (National Examiner, December 24, 2012). This headline appears frequently because it sells. One response to this headline might be "Who cares?" but we, as a culture, care. We have a vested interest in a system that thinks that one can tell the difference between "gay" and "not," and that those differences matter. And if our assumptions about our favorite celebrities are challenged, then our fears are triggered, and our investment in the status quo is challenged.

Exercise

Think of a personal investment you may have in keeping the status quo. It might be in your personal lifestyle, your employment, or cultural traditions.

You might consider your experiences with the global coronavirus pandemic. Many aspects of our lives were altered. How did your life change?

Some of those changes might have been very difficult, and you may have had a sense that they would be challenging as soon as we heard about social distancing. Can you think of any?

Other changes may have presented themselves gradually as being difficult, but you never thought they would be. What were they?

Were there any changes that were positive or enjoyable? Maybe surprisingly so?

Exercise

The following exercise is from: Status Quo Bias: If It Ain't Broke, Why Fix It? Cognitive Bias Series (4:29) (https://academy4sc.org/wp-content/uploads/sites/39/2020/06/Status-Quo-Bias_Lesson-Plan.pdf).

Below is a summary of the video link:

A Deeper Look at Status Quo Bias: Why We Resist Change

People often operate under an unspoken assumption: If things seem to be working, they shouldn't be tampered with. This mindset can feel practical—why disrupt something that appears to be running smoothly? But our instinct to preserve the current state of affairs isn't always rooted in rational thinking. In fact, it's often shaped by a psychological bias known as the **status quo bias**—a deep-seated preference for the familiar over the unfamiliar, even when change could lead to improvement.

Imagine a scenario: A company wants to introduce a new species into a thriving ecosystem. Many would resist this proposal on the grounds that the environment is stable and shouldn't be interfered with. That reaction seems logical and protective. But now picture a different situation: A lake has been polluted for years, and an organization wants to restore it. Surprisingly, people may still resist, insisting that the lake be left alone—simply because it's been that way for a long time.

This resistance stems not from careful reasoning, but from emotional attachment to the way things are. We tend to mistake the familiar for the acceptable, and the unknown for something risky or threatening—even when logic suggests otherwise.

The Psychology Behind the Bias

This inclination is tied to a broader psychological principle called **loss aversion**—the tendency to fear losing something more than we value gaining something of equal or greater value. Applied more generally, this mindset causes people to cling to what they have rather than explore better alternatives.

In decision-making, this often results in a strong pull toward inaction. People feel safer sticking with the known—even if it's flawed—than facing the uncertainty that comes with change. The status quo becomes a kind of comfort zone, regardless of whether it's actually serving us well.

Why This Matters in Real Life

This bias doesn't just affect small personal choices—it shapes our political, social, and financial behavior in meaningful ways:

- **In politics**, voters who haven't deeply engaged with the issues or candidates may default to reelecting familiar leaders. The incumbent feels like the "safe" choice, even when their performance has been poor.
- **In social attitudes**, we see resistance to progress dressed up as nostalgia. Statements like "things were better in the past" often ignore real problems that were simply overlooked or accepted—such as inequality, exclusion, or untreated mental health issues. The belief that past norms should remain untouched can stall necessary improvements.
- **In economics**, status quo bias can lead people to hold onto outdated or underperforming investments out of sentimentality or inertia. Rather

than adapting to new opportunities, they stick with what they've inherited or grown used to—even when the data suggest it's time to move on.

The Risk of Staying Stagnant

Clinging to the current state of things can feel comforting, but it's not always wise. While not every change is inherently good, refusing to question the present just because it's familiar can blind us to real problems and prevent us from embracing positive transformations.

Being aware of this bias allows us to pause, question our gut reactions, and make decisions based on facts and future outcomes—not just habit or fear. Progress depends not just on new ideas, but on our willingness to let go of the old ones when they no longer serve us.

Next, consider these questions (also from the cite above):

1. Name one real-life example of status quo bias that you or someone you know has experienced.
2. What is the most dangerous consequence of the status quo bias that you can think of?
3. In what situations might status quo bias be a positive force in society?

FEAR OF CHANGE

Fear of change is being afraid when emotional and material conditions become different than they once were and is closely associated with investment in the status quo (Thornton, 2016).

For example, if changes occur, what will it mean about how I am seen, evaluated, or ranked in society? How will I understand myself? Being "set in your ways" and avoiding "rocking the boat" are phrases we hear that are related to fear of change (Dottolo, 2019; Bugental & Bugental, 1984).

Here are a few more examples:

> "A strip-mining project forced the citizens of a town in West Germany to be relocated to a similar area nearby. They were offered several options for the plan of their new town. The citizens chose the option most similar to their old town, even though the layout was inefficient and confusing.

When offered several sandwich options for lunch, individuals often choose a sandwich they have eaten before. This phenomenon is called regret avoidance: in seeking to avoid a potential regrettable experience (choosing a new sandwich and disliking it), individuals opt to stick with the status quo (the sandwich with which they are already familiar).

In 1985, Coca Cola unveiled "New Coke," a reformulation of the original Coke flavor. Blind taste tests found that many consumers preferred New Coke to Coke Classic. However, when consumers were given the opportunity to choose which Coke to buy, they chose Coke Classic. New Coke was ultimately discontinued in 1992."

(the previous examples are from Vinney, 2019, https://www.thoughtco.com/status-quo-bias-4172981)

Remember that all of these defense mechanisms show up for everyone at different times in our lives. Fear is often warranted, understandable, and an appropriate reaction to many life events. Sometimes it interferes with our ability to evaluate or respond to different situations. Investment in the status quo and fear of change are very closely connected to one another.

Exercise

Think of a life change that has happened to you or a loved one that invoked your fear of change.

It may be a divorce, change of employment, retirement, or moving to a new community.

What was the change?
What was the fear?
What happened?

Exercise

The following exercise is taken from: Jennifer Sweeton, Copyright © 2019. Trauma Treatment Toolbox. https://www.providence.org/-/media/project/psjh/providence.or/files/behavioral-health/approaching-fear-despite-fear.pdf?rev=16216798e57c499fb9632308e3552fae&hash=B3BA544658CCB597D5FEF86C2190115F

1. Write down a few sentences describing something that you fear doing, but that is also very important to you. For some individuals, this might be practicing assertiveness skills and boundary setting, or applying for a new job.

2. Now, write a few sentences about what you fear about this task, thing, or situation. What does your mind tell you about it that increases your fear? When you think of approaching this situation, what are the thoughts/fears that hold you back?
3. When you imagine these feared outcomes of the feared situation, where do you feel it in your body? What are the sensations that accompany the fear?
4. Next, write down at least three reasons that this feared situation/thing is important to you, despite the fear it produces in you.
5. For a moment, imagine that you have done that feared thing and succeeded. When you imagine success, how do you feel emotionally?
6. Keep imagining what it will be like when you face your fear and succeed. What will you gain from this? List at least three ways that accomplishing this will change your life for the better (even if in very small ways).
7. When you imagine the feeling of success, how does it feel in the body? How are the physical sensations of self-confidence and success different from the sensations of fear?

SHAME

In addition to fear, another significant underlying reason for defensiveness can be shame. Brene Brown (2012) is a researcher who has garnered public attention for her work on shame and vulnerability. Lindsay-Hartz (1984) used the imagery of the mirror to illustrate the psychological function of shame, explaining,

> In shame we view ourselves through the eyes of another, and then realize that we are who we do not want to be and that we cannot now be otherwise. Viewing ourselves through the eyes of another is like looking at ourselves in a mirror. The other person's viewpoint serves as a means for revealing to us a very negative view of ourselves.
>
> *(p. 695)*

While shame is a universal emotion representing a fear of disconnection, of unworthiness, it is also one of the most difficult emotions to discuss (Brown, 2012). Guilt and shame are somewhat overlapping emotions, but guilt is often described as "I feel bad about what I *did*," whereas shame is "I feel bad about who I *am*" (Brown, 2012).

Shame is connected to loneliness and isolation (Bradshaw, 2005). Some people respond to unconscious feelings of shame by lashing out at others. The process of shifting responsibility for causing distress in others can occur by transferring our shame to the individual we have hurt (Amodeo, 2016). The desire to avoid feeling responsible for our behavior can prompt us to want to blame others. Some externalizing responses to shame can appear as rage, criticism, blame, arrogance, contempt, patronizing, and disgust (Bradshaw, 2005; Hendel, 2018). This can lead to a resistance to offer an apology since we can convince ourselves the other person is to blame. Unconscious shame can prevent us from facing mistakes and admitting to being wrong.

Shame can also contribute to a different response by causing us to be overly apologetic and easily yielding in order to deflect criticism (Amodeo, 2016). This can look like a "fawn" response, where we are first to admit a mistake and take the responsibility of being wrong in order to minimize being targeted by others (Bradshaw, 2005). Some internalizing responses to shame can appear as people-pleasing, being "nice," caregiving, addictions, and eating disorders (Bradshaw, 2005). Shame can diminish our self-confidence and weaken social interaction. While everyone feels shame, to feel flawed and searching for strategies to alleviate this emotion may stand in the way of accepting our very own human imperfections.

Shame is an emotion that serves power structures. Some individuals that feel shame and externalize their behaviors end up lashing out against anyone that questions them, defending the status quo. For example, when it is brought to Joe's attention that his comment at work was racist, he responds by saying, "No, *you're* the racist! You are coming after me because I'm white!" Joe lashes out and refuses to participate in the conversation in an adult, open-hearted way. Remember that according to the change triangle, shame serves to prevent Joe from feeling uncomfortable emotions (Hendel, 2018).

Individuals that feel shame and internalize their responses end up turning against themselves, making themselves smaller and yielding to powerful authorities. For example, when it is brought to Sarah's attention that her comment at work was racist, she responds by saying, "Oh my god! I'm so sorry! I'm a terrible person. I wish I wasn't so awful!" Sarah's internalizing also prohibits her from participating in a conversation as a responsible adult and learning from the interaction (Hendel, 2018). Note that these externalizing and internalizing tendencies also tend to be gendered, although that is certainly not always the case. That is, men tend to be discouraged from accepting responsibility, as this is sometimes seen as weak in our culture, while women tend to be encouraged to internalize, precisely for the same reason (Kramer et al., 2008).

SUMMARY

This chapter covers some of the underlying reasons *why* we feel defensive. These reasons can sometimes be the cause of defense mechanisms, or influence the many ways that defensiveness can show up. In-group bias, belief in a just world (or the myth of the meritocracy), investment in the status quo, fear of change, and shame are just some of the psychological dynamics that serve as underpinnings for the many ways we can see defense mechanisms manifest. The next part discusses different types of defense mechanisms. The forms of defensiveness discussed in the following section are not an exhaustive list. There are many different types of defensive behaviors that have been identified in psychological literature (Vaillant, 1992). These different forms overlap and influence each other. The types of defensiveness explored in the next section are those that appear most noticeably in my teaching about "controversial" topics. Now let's turn our attention to different forms of defensiveness so that we can better identify and recognize them when they appear in ourselves and others.

Chapter 3
Recognizing Defensiveness

Darius sits in the dining hall after class, earbuds in, tray untouched. He's replaying something Dr. Felix said during discussion: "Our internalized narratives are shaped by systems, not just experience." It hit hard.

He'd spoken up in class, finally, when they were reading about stereotype threat. He'd said: "Sometimes I wonder if I actually am the stereotype. Like maybe I am too angry. Too defensive."

Dr. Felix had nodded solemnly.

"And where do you think that thought came from?" she had asked. "Whose voice is that in your head?"

He hadn't answered. But now, chewing slowly on his sandwich, he remembers his 9th-grade guidance counselor telling him not to "aim too high" with his college list. He remembers a cop pulling him over for walking home with his hoodie up. He remembers his uncle saying, "Keep your head down. It's not for us to fix."

That voice wasn't his. Not originally.

This chapter explores different ways that defensiveness manifests, or how it shows up in our behaviors. I provide examples in order to illustrate

Transforming Defensiveness: A Guidebook for Rewriting Our Stories & Reclaiming Connection, First Edition. Andrea L. Dottolo.
© 2026 John Wiley & Sons, Inc. All rights reserved, including rights for text and data mining and training of artificial intelligence technologies or similar technologies. Published 2026 by John Wiley & Sons, Inc.

the basic function of the defense mechanism. However, in reality, they can appear much more muddled, where sometimes multiple forms occur simultaneously. Remember that defenses are unconscious, under the surface of our awareness.

Shapiro (2012) provides a useful example of how the unconscious works. She instructs readers to notice the first thought that pops into their head after she offers a single sentence: "Roses are red." Shapiro (2012) states that it is likely that you thought of "Violets are blue." She explains that this is an automatic response. You likely learned these words in childhood. You probably don't remember who taught them to you, or how old you were. You may not have thought about this rhyme in many years. She continues that in examining the sentence, you might also understand that all roses are not red and that violets are not even blue. However, your association between these two phrases is *automatic* and outside of your awareness. Shapiro (2012) summarizes neurological research on the unconscious, stating,

> The automatic reactions that control our emotions come from neural associations within our memory networks that are independent of our higher reasoning power. That's why you can watch in amazement as you do something you know you'll regret later, or get drawn to the wrong people, or feel hurt by someone you have no respect for, or yell at a loved one with little reason, or feel powerless to shake a depression brought on by something that seems inconsequential.
>
> (p. 9)

Our emotional responses are automatically triggered by connections in our memory network that happen outside of our awareness. It is in the process of bringing our unconscious responses into our awareness that we can choose how to respond to them accordingly. We cannot change what we cannot see.

DENIAL

Denial "occurs when people refuse to admit that something unpleasant is happening" (Wade & Tavris, 2012, p. 43). Denial protects us from what we do not want to see, simultaneously absolving us from responsibility of any wrongdoing (Dorpat, 1985; Matias, 2018). For example, some people claim that racial injustice is a thing of the past (Dunn & Nelson, 2011), that "it's all over now," sometimes accompanied with relief that since African Americans now occupy some top positions in business, government, and more, we no longer have to consider the institutional, cultural, and social impacts of racism.

Denial is sometimes a response to global warming. The Intergovernmental Panel on Climate Change informs us, "Scientific evidence for warming of the climate system is unequivocal" (https://climate.nasa.gov/evidence/), yet some people respond with "that's not true!" (Kemp et al., 2010). It is often easier, safer, far more calming to deny these challenging problems than to address the complicated possible solutions and confront our own difficult emotional responses. One response to this rebuttal is to consider, "okay, but what might it mean for us if it is true? What is at stake for us?"

Sometimes denial functions to protect us from very personal tragedies. The first step in most recovery programs is admitting that there is a problem. If a friend of mine notices my son's alcohol problem and alludes to the fact that he might be an addict, I might vehemently refuse, strongly disagree, and maybe even stop associating with my friend altogether. My denial protects me from my fear, shame, sadness, fury, disappointment, and helplessness I will likely feel if I face the fact of my son's addiction (Wing, 1995). In this instance, facing the truth represents a threat, the angry bear, that we may likely want to deny.

It is also important to remember that defenses like denial are often under the surface, outside our awareness, in our unconscious (Freud, 1923). We are often not aware that we are in denial. Denial is our mind's way of protecting us, making us believe the untruth. It is our lizard brain taking over, "deciding" to react in an automatic and defensive way since our wizard brain has gone offline, retreating from the threatening information (Hammond, 2014; Troncale, 2014).

Once, while teaching about Freudian stages of development, we were discussing psychosexual stages and gender identity, and his idea that children learn to identify with a caregiver of the same gender (Ryckman, 2008). In a discussion of gender roles, a woman student expressed confusion, asserting that men are "naturally" aggressive, while women are "natural" caretakers, and stated, "I thought aggression was about testosterone." Another woman student (who was writing a thesis about aggression) responded, "Well, we used to think that, but now we know it's more about social norms." The original student continued to be confused and mentioned that when boys become teenagers that they "naturally" become more aggressive. When the class turned to me, I provided an example to illustrate that gender varies dramatically across cultures, including in the Aka, a group living in Central Africa. Aka men are often central caretakers of children, often nursing infants by breastfeeding (Fouts et al., 2012; Hewlett & Winn, 2014; Moses et al., 2021). The original student became visibly agitated and cried out, "That's not true! That's disgusting!"

This example illustrates how denial can arise in connection with several emotions all at once, perhaps for this student including surprise, disgust, confusion, and anger. This student also expressed a reliance on "biological law" (with her claims about what is "natural") which we will discuss later. As you can see, there can be multiple forces operating at once in moments of defensiveness.

Denial can also be connected to *cognitive dissonance*, one of the concepts we discussed earlier (Aronson, 1969). Since we might struggle to hold two contradictory beliefs at the same time, we choose the one that is less scary. For example, it might make me uncomfortable to consider the ways that racism continues to be ever present in our culture, so I'd rather just decide that "it's all over now." Or, a smoker convinces themselves that "smoking isn't that bad" in order to reduce the psychological tension caused by their awareness of the health risks. Or, in the aforementioned example, the student could not reconcile that women could also engage in a practice that is outside her understanding of cultural gender norms, so she chose to defend a "position," while disparaging another culture.

You might know someone who always says that they are "fine," even when it is clear that they are struggling. They might be struggling emotionally, psychologically, or physically, but they refuse to admit or acknowledge it at all. It is likely that they never learned how to process difficult emotions, and/or that revealing any form of "weakness" was unsafe. Denial helps them not only to avoid the uncomfortable emotions, but also head off any real or imagined punishment. However, you can see how denial keeps a person "stuck" in their feelings, and perhaps also in the problem or situation that created the uncomfortable emotions.

If I deny that my son is an alcoholic, then I can never help him. As I deny my son's alcohol addiction, remember that the change triangle (Hendel, 2018) helps us to understand how denial protects us from feeling *core emotions* (in this case, fear, anger, and sadness) and also *inhibitory emotions* (anxiety, guilt, and shame). However, the price to pay for this protection is great, since it also prevents me from feeling the 8 Cs: calmness, curiosity, clarity, compassion, confidence, courage, creativity and connectedness (Schwartz & Sweezy, 2020). If I deny the health risks of drinking alcohol, I will face both the short- and long-term consequences for my behaviors.

Exercise

Can you think of a time when you noticed someone else's denial? What do you think they found difficult to accept?

Can you think of a time when you noticed your own denial? What do you think you found difficult to accept? Try these steps:

Step 1: Observe Denial

For example, perhaps I gained 10 pounds in the past few months. I might ask myself, what am I in denial about? How can I be careful not to judge or harshly criticize myself? In other words, I want to avoid statements like, "I have no self-control! I'm a loser. I'll always be fat. I can't do this." Instead, how can I try to notice, perceive my own behavior as simply a witness? Perhaps I have had slightly larger portions lately, or eating late-night snacks, eating out more often, or even drinking alcohol.

Step 2: Identify Feelings

What have I been feeling when I have been in a state of denial? What emotions have contributed to me going off track in my eating plan? Worry? Fear? Overwhelmed? Exhaustion? Notice how my denial has served to distract me from my feelings, preventing me from having to look at them (Hendel, 2018).

Step 3: Identify Needs

What needs were not being met, that I attempted to address with food? Relaxation? Sleep? Needing alone time? Needing to slow down?

Step 4: Request

How can I fulfill my needs in some way other than food? How can I create time for relaxing? How can I request of myself to pay attention to my needs and address them by slowing down?

Notice that once I can address my feelings and behaviors directly, I can function from a more grounded, open-hearted place (Hendel, 2018). This open-heartedness allows me to not only tend to myself and my own needs, but helps me to be a better, healthier, more empathic person to the people in my life. When I engage in denial and sabotage, I tend to be a more unhappy person in a variety of ways, perhaps including feeling irritable, sad, lonely, shameful, resentful, and angry, all of which are bound to spill out onto the people I love.

(These steps taken from https://www.youtube.com/watch?v=7P2lJw_M4qI)

AVOIDANCE

Avoidance, like denial, involves evading unpleasant or threatening information (Cramer, 2000). When we encounter information or situations that we find threatening, we may engage in avoidance by not going to certain places, or not doing particularly unpleasant activities (Dottolo, 2019). For example, sometimes I see a commercial or ad for a charity for starving children in an impoverished village of an "underdeveloped" nation. When I first see the images of poverty and despair, I feel guilty, angry, scared, and powerless all at the same time. To avoid feeling this way, I change the channel, close the window, or click on something else, and evade the negative emotions by avoiding the commercial entirely.

Procrastination is another version of avoidance (Fee & Tangney, 2000). When I know I have an unpleasant task to accomplish, like doing the laundry, sometimes I just say, "I'll do it tomorrow" as a way to avoid having to do it today. Or, I might even chase that task away by doing a slightly less aversive task, that I have also been trying to avoid. I might say to myself, "Instead of doing the laundry, I will pay bills." This will allow me to feel accomplished by having paid bills, while I was able to avoid carrying heavy bundles of laundry.

Avoidance is different than denial. For example, "I know that I have to do the laundry, I just don't want to do it," so I find a way to escape it. Denial is the refusal to admit something unpleasant, so in this case it might be, "I don't have any laundry—all my clothes are clean," even though there is a big heap of dirty laundry in my room.

One study (Fee & Tangney, 2000) found that shame was especially related to procrastination, especially as it is also connected to perfectionism. "People who are vulnerable to the ugly feeling of shame and who believe that others expect them to be perfect, are especially likely to procrastinate on important tasks" (Fee & Tangney, 2000, p. 182). This study investigated college student behavior around avoiding academic tasks. However, the researchers also mention everyday unpleasant tasks such as making necessary phone calls, having your car serviced, and running errands. Remember that shame is a global negative evaluation of the self, so it makes sense then that someone might want to protect their self-image through procrastination, which is a kind of avoidance.

Avoidance is basically when we "look the other way," away from something that makes us feel uncomfortable. A person who has recently lost their job might distract themselves from their sadness, anger, or anxiety by "keeping busy." This is not to say that sometimes distraction can be a useful tool, especially when our emotions are intense and strong. Using distraction as a temporary way to self-regulate is healthy. Distraction is not necessarily avoidance because you know you need to take a step away from a problem or conversation with the intent to return when you are in a calmer state. Avoidance is when you turn away, not necessarily with the intention to address the situation. We might binge-watch shows or movies, overwork on other projects or hobbies, or engage in excessive socializing or partying.

Remember that denial is different from avoidance. In this example, the person who lost their job is aware of the problem and is sad and angry about it, as well as being scared about how they will pay their bills. They avoid these feelings and the daunting task of dealing with their finances and searching for a new job. Someone who was in denial would say, "I didn't lose my job. Everything is fine." Denial refuses to admit, whereas avoidance evades. While avoidance serves to temporarily protect us from our *core and inhibitory emotions* (Hendel, 2018), the longer we avoid, the larger the problem can become.

Exercise

Construct a list of places or situations that you avoid. At the top of the list put those places or situations which make you most anxious. At the bottom of the ladder put places or situations you avoid, but which don't bother you as much. In the middle of the ladder put ones that are "in-between." Give each item a rating from 0% to 100% according to how anxious you would feel if you had to be in that situation (https://www.psychologytools.com/resource/avoidance-hierarchy/).

Situation	Anxiety (0–100%)

Remember that avoidance is just another form of protection and that sometimes it serves us and sometimes it does not. This exercise might help you to identify how avoidance and anxiety are connected to one another. This is an important link to understand the relationship between our feelings and behaviors, especially our (perhaps) unconscious reactions.

MINIMIZATION

Minimization is when we respond to a threat by making it seem smaller than it is, thus making it more manageable. If we return to the idea of a threat being represented as an angry grizzly bear ready to attack, we try to turn the big, snarling bear into a cute, tiny teddy bear so that it seems less scary.

In the global coronavirus pandemic, many people first reacted to the reports by minimizing the extent and deadliness of the virus (Ries, 2022). Many people initially minimized the impact of the pandemic, believing the numbers of deaths were inflated, risks were low in transmitting the disease, and wearing masks was not necessary (Islam et al., 2020). This was a global crisis laden with understandable fear and anxiety, and the minimization of it attempted to calm and reassure the public, and also themselves. Trying to reduce the problem led to a lack of action, especially in the United States, resulting in many illnesses and deaths throughout the world (Miller, 2020). By minimizing the problem, we also minimized the responsibility for taking appropriate action and seeking solutions. In this way, trying to make the problem smaller actually made it much bigger.

Minimizing is a common reaction when a situation or event causes distress and negativity (Yilmaz, 2024). One way to decrease the emotional impact of a negative event is, for example, to downplay the significance of a rude remark, a disappointing social encounter, or the accomplishment you may have hoped for but not achieved. A hurtful remark or insult can be minimized by claiming it was meant as a joke, or an offhanded unintentional comment. A strong emotional reaction is avoided with this dismissal. Minimizing can be a defense mechanism used when feelings or shame or guilt are present. The father who lost his temper and yelled at his young child may feel ashamed and guilty, but dismisses his actions as merely speaking in a loud voice, not yelling at his youngster. Patients might minimize worrisome cholesterol test results as "no big deal" (Croyle et al., 1993).

Minimizing can also be used to downplay our accomplishments. In an attempt to present ourselves as modest individuals, not wanting to brag, we might minimize our skills, abilities, and effort put into personal achievements.

This is often displayed by women who are socialized to be modest (Smith & Huntoon, 2014). The response of minimizing personal abilities and successes might indicate a struggle with self-worth, feelings of inferiority, and low self-esteem. The excellent grade received on a test may be attributed to just luck and good guessing. Minimizing both the good and bad distorts and twists reality. It remakes what is true.

Smith and Huntoon (2014) share an example:

> Several years ago, we were putting together a magazine featuring the achievements of women faculty on campus. We put out a call for women to share their successes and accomplishments in teaching or research or family life. We received no replies. We did, however, receive many replies from people telling us about other women we should feature and the good work that these other women on campus were doing. Examples such as ours illustrate that many women are fine with referencing the good works of others but are reticent to promote themselves.

While unwilling to promote themselves, the women Smith and Huntoon (2014) discuss were happy to give praise to others. By minimizing their personal good work, women prevent their own advancement and success in professional careers and personal endeavors. U.S. culture often requires self-promotion and willingness to openly acknowledge our abilities and skills. Gender modesty and stereotyping require women to be selfless, quiet, unpretentious, and willing to deny their successes but accepting of failure. When women step out of these cultural expectations and advocate for themselves, it is breaking out of the norm and can cause anxiety, nervousness, or even fear (Smith & Huntoon, 2014). In an effort to avoid these negative emotions, it is more comfortable to deny self-promoting, downplay successes, and adhere to the strategy of minimizing and conforming to the modesty norm.

There are many gendered examples of minimization. For example, gender stereotypes and norms dictate that men are allowed to be angry, but never sad, while women can be sad, but never angry (Plant et al., 2000). Women often experience minimization as a response to their anger, being told to "calm down," or "relax," that their emotions are "too big," "too much," and that they should be emotionally smaller (Cherry, 2019). Men tend to experience minimization in response to their fear, sadness, or any expression that is deemed by the culture to show vulnerability (Cherry, 2019).

Another form of minimization is *unintentionality*. This is a defense when one claims that they "didn't mean it" in response to a harm that they knowingly commit. Unintentionality is a much more conscious, aware defense than many of the others. For example, you may have heard someone say, "well, he didn't *mean* to hurt her when he punched her." Or, "look, I don't mean to be rude, I just don't like gay people—no offense." In this case, the use of the phrase "no offense" indicates that the speaker is indeed aware that their statement might be insulting or inappropriate. This statement is how we can observe specific behavior that suggests awareness. You may have heard someone say something like, "I couldn't help but stare at the woman in the wheelchair… what else was I supposed to do?" This also attempts to shift blame away from the speaker by making it seem as though there were no other options. Sometimes we hear this in the phrase at the end of a statement like, "… I'm just saying …" such as: "I just don't think transgender people should have rights … I'm just saying." This makes it seem as though simply ("just") making an utterance is somehow neutral or value free. The speaker also clearly understands that their statement is not objective or without harm, or they would not need to qualify it as such. In each of these cases, the individual uses the excuse of "not meaning it" to minimize any potential harm.

Introspective/Journaling Exercise

Can you think of a time when your own experiences were minimized by someone else? Perhaps you expressed a feeling or a concern about something, and someone told you that "you are making a big deal out of nothing," or "that's ridiculous." What happened?

How did their response make you feel?

Can you think of a time when you may have minimized someone else's experience? Perhaps they expressed a feeling or a concern about something, and you told them that they were "making a big deal out of nothing," or "that's ridiculous." What happened?

Exercise

Can you think of a time when your own experiences were minimized by someone else? Perhaps you expressed a feeling or a concern about something, and someone told you that "you are making a big deal out of nothing," or "that's ridiculous." What happened?

How did their response make you feel?

Can you think of a time when you may have minimized someone else's experience? Perhaps they expressed a feeling or a concern about something, and you told them that they were "making a big deal out of nothing," or "that's ridiculous." What happened?

RATIONALIZATION

Another way to excuse or downsize our discomfort is through *rationalization*. This involves inventing a "plausible" explanation for acts or opinions that are actually based on other causes that an individual finds difficult to accept (Buunk & Dijkstra, 2001). The tendency to invent an explanation or excuse that sounds more acceptable alleviates guilt, fear, and anxiety, or any other negative emotions that might arise as a result of facing the reality of a situation.

An incorrect rationalization as a response to police shootings is to "justify" them by "explaining" that "African Americans steal" (Michael Brown was accused of stealing cigars) (Mirzoeff, 2016) and since the police need to reduce crime, their responses are "understandable." Some people may be surprised to learn that White women, especially teenagers, comprise the demographic that is most likely to shoplift. "In fact … more than two thirds of the shoplifters apprehended in this nation are White females" (Asquith & Bristow, 2000, p. 273). Yet, most retailers do not racially profile White teenage girls. In this example, we rationalize the actions of the police by explaining that their behavior was justified, even though the "reason" is not substantiated by verifiable evidence.

I might rationalize my alcohol consumption by telling myself that the benefits outweigh the costs. I might say that a glass of wine will help me live longer, or it relaxes me, or "it's only one drink!" This is an attempt for me to "explain away" the compelling counterevidence that alcohol, in fact, does not reduce mortality (Fillmore et al., 2006; Naimi et al., 2017). In fact, alcohol *causes* anxiety (Allan, 1995; Wilson, 1988). Furthermore, there is no amount of alcohol that is considered safe (Burton & Sheron, 2018; GBD Alcohol Collaborators, 2018; Rabin, 2025). Alcohol is intertwined into American culture such that we often rationalize that since "everybody does it," then it must be safe. However, research clearly tells us that it is not.

I might use rationalization to justify that my clothes are too tight that they were shrunk in the wash or dry cleaner. This explanation allows me to avoid considering my weight gain as a result of my food choices and habits.

According to the change triangle (Hendel, 208), rationalization prevents me from an open-hearted state, keeping me stuck in trying to fight what I see as a threat, or the "bear." If I can package my argument with a pretty little bow that makes it sound like a good story, then I can use it as an excuse. I might be justifying bad behavior (either mine or someone else's), but most importantly, I am making a "good reason," a "plausible explanation" to stick to the story that makes me feel less bad.

Exercise

When white women were fighting for the right to vote in the United States up through the twentieth century, some folks argued that they should not be allowed to vote because it is "not a woman's place," and "they will only vote how their husbands instruct them to vote anyway." Why was this a rationalization against women's suffrage? What feelings (and whom) were being protected?

Exercise: Identifying Rationalization in Personal Behavior

Step 1: Select a Recent Situation

Think about a recent situation where you acted in a way that you later felt uncertain, guilty, or conflicted. This could involve a decision at work, a personal interaction, a financial choice, or any moment where your behavior didn't fully align with your values or intentions.

Describe the situation in detail. Write about:

- What happened?
- What did you do or say?
- What was the outcome of the situation?

Step 2: Identify Your Initial Thoughts and Justifications

Reflect on your immediate thoughts after the event. Did you justify or explain your actions to yourself or others? Often, rationalization occurs quickly as a way to reduce internal discomfort.

Write down any justifications or explanations you gave for your behavior, no matter how logical or reasonable they might seem.

Example

- "I didn't really have any other choice."
- "I had to do that because if I didn't, something worse would have happened."
- "It wasn't really my fault; I was just trying to make things easier."

Step 3: Dig Deeper—Uncover the Emotions Behind the Rationalization

Now, explore how your rationalization was an attempt to cover up underlying emotions like fear, guilt, shame, or frustration.

- What emotions were you trying to avoid by justifying your behavior?
- How might your actions have been influenced by things like personal insecurities, anxiety, or past experiences?
- What might you have done differently if you didn't feel the need to justify your actions?
- Could the real reason for your behavior involve something like fear of judgment, wanting to avoid conflict, or prioritizing personal convenience over others' needs?

Step 4: Confront the Truth

In this final step, take some time to be honest with yourself about the situation. What might it reveal about your values, priorities, or internal conflicts? How can you grow from this insight? How can you apply what you've learned to make more aligned choices in the future?

Rationalization is a common defense mechanism we use to protect ourselves from uncomfortable truths. By recognizing when we're rationalizing and gently challenging those justifications, we can move toward greater self-awareness and growth. This exercise can be repeated periodically to help build that awareness and deepen your understanding of your inner motivations.

BLAMING THE VICTIM

Blaming the victim occurs when we hold responsible or at fault the person who has been harmed or mistreated (Ryan, 2010). It involves redirecting or displacing anger onto the target of injustice. Most of us are very familiar with this form of defensiveness, most often in response to sexual violence (Dottolo, 2019). Sometimes when we hear about a woman who was raped, we conclude that she must have been "asking for it." Frequently folks ask questions such as, "What was she wearing?" or "What was doing out with him at that time of night?" or "How much did she drink?" or "Why was she in that part of town, anyway?" The belief that "she should have known better" is a way to blame the victim. These are questions not only asked by everyday people, but by many authorities, including the police.

In general, as a culture, we tend to respond by blaming the victim around many acts of violence targeted at marginalized people. This is a direct consequence of the belief in a just world. If we believe that good things happen to those that are good, then bad things must happen to those that are bad, that they deserved it somehow. For example, in response to domestic violence, we sometimes hear, "well, if she just kept her mouth shut, then she wouldn't get hit." Or, when Matthew Shepard was murdered in 1998 for being gay, many folks reacted by saying, "well he was in a gay bar, what did he expect?" Matthew Shepard's killers specifically targeted the gay bar. In fact, they pretended to be gay in order to lure him away from the bar to murder him (Hawkins, 2025; Sheerin, 2018).

Another example of blaming the victim involves attitudes about mental illness. Forty-three percent of Americans think that people who have a mental illness "bring it on themselves," 35% think it is a "punishment for sinful behavior," and 19% point to "lack of willpower or self-discipline" (Comer, 2010). Other researchers have also examined the relationships between blame, stigma, and mental illness (Galanis & King, 2025; Patterson et al., 2025; Twiss et al., 2025). As an extension of a belief in a just world, if we focus all our attention on the victim, then we never have to consider the individuals or systems that might also be responsible for the negative outcome.

Blaming the victim is especially toxic and works in multiple ways. If we take the example of rape (and I am speaking in great generality and stereotype here), men might blame women who are victims as a way to not have to question their own behaviors. At some level, this is understandable, since individuals who already hold power want to protect themselves from being accused of any wrongdoing.

However, it is not just men who blame survivors of rape. Many women also point the finger at other women, also attributing their fate to their own behaviors: "she didn't have to go up to his room," and "why she would dress like that?" In this way, potential targets blame the victim in order to protect themselves from threat, so that "if *I* don't dress like that, or behave like that, then it won't happen to *me*." Of course, we know that what one wears or how they behave is entirely unrelated to sexual violence (Griffin, 1971; Harding, 2015), but it serves as a way to provide a sense of security, of control, that I might be able to protect myself.

Therefore, when sexual violence inevitably does happen to us, we internalize this idea. We know that the numbers of women and transgender people who have endured sexual violence is staggering (Coulter et al., 2017; Eustaquio et al., 2025; Johnson, 1980; Wilson & Miller, 2016) and while we are just learning more about men who are victims, those statistics are always higher than any report, precisely because of this stigma. So, when we *are* victimized, we turn this logic inward, asking ourselves "Why did I wear that?" We blame ourselves, with conclusions like, "I shouldn't have let him walk me home. I deserved it." The shame and tragedy of blaming the victim only leads to silence, denial, depression, suicide, and the legacy and cycle of abuse (Dorahy, 2017; Hastings et al., 2002; Kim et al., 2011). This defense mechanism is especially powerful and automatic. Remember that we all use it at some time or another, against others, or with ourselves.

We have heard and read opinions regarding "blaming the victim" in cases of individuals struggling with poverty (Ryan, 1976). You may have heard the sentiment that "those people" need to work harder, get an education, stop having children that they cannot afford, and generally make better choices since it is their own fault they are impoverished (Wright, 1993). This is often a common psychological and societal response when viewing poverty (Kaplan, 2012). If we consider the structural and systemic societal issues that cause inequity in our system, it makes it clear that poverty and other miseries are greatly dependent on issues of racism, segregation, sexism that are deeply ingrained into victim blaming, and into the human tendency to use this defense mechanism to make ourselves feel safe and secure (Assari, 2017). The social barriers with which marginalized groups deal daily causes disparity in education, employment, and opportunities taken for granted by the majority (Assari, 2017). The social structures both obvious and subtle reinforce the human tendency to blame the victim, putting most or part of the blame for their misfortune on them. Much research (Ferriss, 2006; McEwen & McEwen, 2017; Ogujiuba et al., 2011; Wilson, 2010) provides an alternative understanding of poverty, that it is often caused by environmental and historical issues raising the need to be wary of placing blame on the individual (Assari, 2017).

Sometimes individuals identify with stereotypes associated with their group membership.

Myths and untruths that society communicates about their group become part of the individual's belief system and self-image. Working class and poor people may believe they can only do menial work and are less worthy than more privileged members of society (Yurdakul & Atik, 2016). Women may believe the myth that they are inherently not good at math or participating in the sciences (Pratiwi, 2018). Within communities of color, individuals might internalize societal preferences for lighter skin tones, leading to discrimination or prejudice against those with darker skin within the same group (Dixon & Telles, 2017). When groups are told misinformation, myths, and stereotypical characterizations regarding the people with which they identify, these beliefs can become internalized. Often the harmful self-perceptions can be unconscious, and subtly reinforced by others.

This internalization of stereotypes can not only be within the individual, but within a group. Michelle Obama (2021) describes in her book *Becoming* that as a young girl of ten, she was challenged by another black child for "talking like a white girl" (p. 40). She explains that she felt she was "perceived as a betrayal, as being uppity, as somehow denying our culture" (Obama, 2021, p. 40). In his movie *School Days* (1989), Spike Lee highlights how light-skinned Black students considered darker skinned classmates as inferior because of the color of their skin. These examples demonstrate how people of color take in and accept ideas of those in power and make them their own, applying these beliefs to themselves and others in their communities (David et al., 2019).

Blaming the victim is related to the belief in a just world because it represents how the American Dream explains away negative experiences. According to the myth, "good things happen to good people who work hard, and bad things happen to bad people who are lazy." Therefore, as a way to align ourselves with the power structures, the systems that depend upon us endorsing these ideas, we absorb the ideas into our psyche. If something bad happens, if we are mistreated, according to the logic, we must have "deserved it." We assimilate our beliefs to match the system that we hold dear, even if it hurts us. Gloria Yamato (1990) explains,

> Internalized racism is what really gets in my way as a Black woman. It influences the way I see or don't see myself, limits what I expect of myself or others like me. It results in my acceptance of mistreatment, leads me to believe that being treated with less than absolute respect, at least this once, is to be expected because I am Black, because I am not white.
>
> (p. 2)

Remember that *internalization* is also a tendency in managing our defenses, as compared to *externalization* (Gibson, 2015). While internalizing can be painful and difficult, it serves to protect us from what could potentially be real danger.

For example, there are not many possible pathways for a woman of color to resist systemic racism without facing emotional, psychological, and physical violence in response. The brutality she might endure could come from individuals and systems both inside and outside her community. Furthermore, social structures are invested in all of us buying into these ideas so that we all are "kept in our place."

Exercise

Now let's consider the following question. List as many answers as you can, just from the top of your head.

Why do *some students* drop out of school?

List your answers here:

Now look at your answers. Do you think your answers focus on the reason for some students dropping out of school at the level of the individual or a broader societal reason?

Now answer the following question in the same way, just from what you already know.

Why do *some schools* have such high dropout rates?

List your answers here:

Now look at your answers. Do you think your answers focus on the reason for some schools having high dropout rates at the level of the individual or a broader societal reason?

Do you notice any similarities and differences between your two lists?

This exercise can draw out explanations for social problems that blame the individual, or alternatively, can elicit answers which also take social systems into account. The way the question is phrased can determine the answers we provide. For example, some people explain why *some students* drop out of school due to pregnancy, loss of a job, or caring for a sick parent or child. These are individual problems or responsibilities. While many might include those same reasons for the following question, some responses to why *some schools* have such high dropout rates include poverty, low minimum wage, or lack of access to healthcare, which locate the responsibility for the problem in a larger social context, not just on the individual.

Ask yourself, which question would you want a social worker to ask? A teacher? A state legislator? Why? If you are in a "helping" profession, how do the questions you ask influence how we understand and solve problems?

As a culture, we tend to ask the individual version of the question, again, often because of our investment in the American Dream.

Scenario Exercise: Understanding Blaming the Victim

Amara works as a cashier at a busy retail store. One day, she's working her shift when a customer begins to raise his voice and demand a refund for a faulty product. Despite Amara trying to handle the situation calmly and professionally, the customer continues to get angrier, accusing her of being unhelpful and rude.

The store manager, Rosa, overhears the exchange and comes over. After the customer leaves, she says to Amara, "You really need to learn how to deal with customers better. If you were more patient and polite, things wouldn't have escalated like that. You need to be more attentive to customers' needs and avoid making them upset."

Amara is confused and hurt by the manager's words. She did everything she could to stay calm and follow protocol. The customer was the one who started the confrontation, yet the blame is placed on her.

Questions for Reflection

1. **Blaming the Victim in Action:** In this scenario, how is Amara being blamed for something that wasn't her fault? Why is it unfair to place the blame on Amara? What role did the customer play in the situation that isn't being acknowledged? Why is that being ignored in favor of blaming Amara?
2. **Alternative Interpretation:** How might Rosa handle this situation differently if she recognized that Amara was simply trying to do her job while the customer was being unreasonable?
3. If you were Amara, how would you feel about being blamed for something outside of your control? How might this situation affect your trust in the management or your feelings of job satisfaction?

Debriefing:

- Blaming the victim occurs when the person who is suffering or being mistreated is held responsible for their own victimization, rather than recognizing the real cause or responsibility behind the situation.

- In this case, Amara is unjustly blamed for an escalation that was largely the customer's fault, and the lack of acknowledgment of the customer's behavior shows how easily victim-blaming can occur.
- Recognizing and challenging victim-blaming can help create a more supportive and just environment, where individuals are held accountable for their actions rather than projecting blame onto the wrong person.

PROJECTION

Projection is when we accuse someone else of our own uncomfortable thoughts, feelings, or behaviors (Freud, 1923). In other words, we ascribe or blame our unacceptable emotions or actions on another person (Cramer, 2015). Think of a movie projector that "projects" an image on a screen. Similarly, we take our "icky" feelings and throw them onto someone else. For example, if you are really angry at someone, you might accuse *them* of being mad at *you*.

Remember that we all engage in projection sometimes. In order to protect ourselves from confronting difficult emotions and impulses, we instead shift the burden to another person. This is an obvious example of *externalizing* (Gibson, 2015), where we "throw" our negative feelings outside ourselves. For instance, your boss might accuse you of being a "slacker" on a project when they are the one that consistently leaves work early and does not follow through on their tasks.

Remember that projection is largely unconscious, happening underneath the surface of the "iceberg," outside our awareness (Freud, 1923). By accusing someone else of our negative feelings or behaviors, we avoid responsibility. For example, someone might feel guilty about their dishonesty and accuse someone else of lying. By locating conflict or emotion outside ourselves, we reduce internal stress (Claney, 2024).

Projection can also function to reinforce our worldviews (Claney, 2024). I might assume that "everyone" shares my racist beliefs. We can see how this assumption serves to uphold power structures. Our individual psychological defense also works to make sure that institutional systems stay in place. Another powerful example of projection on a group level is connected to attitudes toward sexuality and religiosity, specifically Christians. Research shows that higher amounts of pornography are consumed by the Bible Belt states in the United States (Burke, 2016; Whitehead & Perry, 2018). This illustrates an idea that can represent projection: that every accusation is a confession. In other words, when someone vehemently opposes a group or issue, it is often a mask for their own hidden or unconscious feelings. Some Christians have conservative, rigid beliefs about sexuality, including sex outside of marriage, birth control, and pornography. It makes sense then, that their staunch, fierce positions about sexuality serves to counteract their actual feelings about sexuality. They "throw" their own feelings onto others who are "sinners." This internalization of a group message serves to uphold the power structure of religious control.

Or, to quote Shakespeare (1992/1604), thou "doth protest too much."

Scenario Exercise: Understanding Projection

Scenario

Isabella and Maria are roommates. Isabella has been feeling overwhelmed by her responsibilities lately—work is demanding, she's trying to maintain a social life, and she's also been struggling with her mental health. She finds herself snapping at Maria more often, even when Maria hasn't done anything wrong.

One day, after a small disagreement about chores, Isabella says, "You never listen to me! You always ignore my needs and expect me to do everything around here. I can't take it anymore."

In reality, Isabella has been neglecting her own self-care and hasn't communicated clearly with Maria about her needs. She's been feeling resentful but hasn't addressed her own stress or the imbalance of responsibilities she's facing. Instead, she projects these unspoken feelings onto Maria, blaming her for things that are actually stemming from Isabella's own struggles.

Questions for Reflection

1. **Projection in Action**: How is Isabella using projection in this situation? What feelings or needs might she be attributing to Maria that are actually her own?
2. **Unconscious Motivation**: Why does Isabella attribute blame to Maria rather than addressing her own emotions or communicating her needs? What is she avoiding by doing this?
3. **Alternative View**: If Isabella were able to reflect on her own feelings of stress and exhaustion, how might she interpret Maria's actions differently? How could this change their relationship and communication?

4. **Self-Reflection**: What steps could Isabella take to express herself more openly with Maria and reduce feelings of resentment?

Debriefing:
- Projection occurs when someone unconsciously transfers their own feelings, flaws, or struggles onto others. In this case, Isabella's stress and lack of communication are being projected as Maria's behavior.
- Recognizing projection can help prevent unnecessary conflict and promote healthier communication. Isabella could benefit from taking time to understand and address her own feelings before reacting or blaming others.

Exercise

Can you think of a time when you "blamed" *someone else* for your feelings? What happened?

Can you think of a time when someone else "blamed" *you* for what seemed to be *their* feelings? What happened?

REPRESSION

The term repression comes from the idea to "hold back" or "hold down." Freud first described repression as a way the mind keeps painful memories out of our conscious awareness (Freud, 1953). This happens when a memory is so distressing—like imagining an angry bear chasing you—that your brain protects you by hiding the memory completely. For example, many people who survived war might have large gaps in memory about what happened to them because their minds hid these painful experiences (Banks, 2011; Rivers, 1918).

Repression often shows up in people who have gone through extreme trauma, such as survivors of sexual violence or childhood abuse (Herman, 2015; Krahé, 1999). These individuals may seem to forget parts of their past, even though the feelings—like emotions or fear—may resurface later, through vivid nightmares or distressing dreams (Herman, 2015; Van der Kolk, 2014). This forgetting is the brain's way of protecting itself from terrifying memories that could disrupt everyday life.

You might not notice someone's repression directly, but it can appear in how they act. Someone might react in a very defensive way when asked about a certain topic, even though they don't know why. This can be a clue that something painful is buried deep in their mind. For instance, a person who feels attracted to someone they shouldn't—like a teacher or a friend's partner—might repress that feeling out of shame, even though it still affects their thoughts and behavior.

In thinking about the change triangle, Hendel (2018) explains that defenses like repression are often supported by inhibitory emotions, particularly shame and anxiety. Someone who experienced childhood abuse might repress the memory to avoid feelings of shame or helplessness. In this way, repression and inhibitory emotions work together to block access to the truth of one's emotional experience (Hendel, 2018; Herman, 2015). These blocked emotions might later show up in nightmares, body symptoms, or outbursts that seem disconnected from any clear cause (Van der Kolk, 2014). This illustrates how repression, while self-protective in the short term, may limit healing if not eventually brought into awareness.

Using the change triangle, therapists aim to help clients identify when they're using a defense like repression and slowly guide them toward the core emotions that were too overwhelming to feel earlier in life. This might include creating safety to name the repressed material, feel the associated emotions (grief, fear, anger), and ultimately process them in a supported setting. For example, a client working through childhood trauma may gradually become aware of previously inaccessible memories or feelings. As they process these core emotions with compassion, they move toward the bottom of the triangle, where emotional healing and clarity are possible (Della Selva, 2018; Hendel, 2018).

Case Study 3.1
SCENARIO

Elena is a 30-year-old woman who, for as long as she can remember, has struggled with an intense fear of dogs. She has no memory of being bitten as a child, but as an adult, she panics if a dog comes near. In therapy, she doesn't deliberately think about any past event—her mind seems blank on the topic. One night, she dreams of a small, fierce dog barking and chasing her down a hallway. She wakes up terrified. When she talks about the dream, she suddenly recalls being attacked by a neighbor's dog as a toddler—something she never knew she remembered.

> **ANALYSIS**
> Elena's fear is an example of repression at work. Her brain hid the memory of the dog attack to protect her young self. The memory resurfaced later through a nightmare. This shows how repression can shield someone from immediate pain, but may also cause ongoing fears that make life harder. Therapy helped her connect the dream to her real experience.

Reflective Exercise
Step 1: Think of a Time
Have you ever reacted strongly to something—like a sound, smell, or place—and felt worried but didn't know why? Describe that memory.

Step 2: Write or Draw
- What do you think your mind might have been protecting you from?
- Can you imagine a hidden memory or emotion behind your reaction?

Step 3: Discussion or Quiet Reflection
- How do dreams, slips of the tongue, or strong reactions help us learn what is repressed inside?
- Why might repression be both protective and yet hold us back at the same time?

Exercise
Can you list three examples of repression depicted in a television show or movie?
   (Hint: Think of situations where people forget trauma, avoid confronting fears, or fail to recall distressing memories.)

Scenario Exercise
A person was involved in a car accident when they were a child. Over the years, they completely forgot about the event and do not feel any distress when hearing about car accidents. However, they sometimes have unexplained anxiety around driving.

- How might repression be at play in this scenario?
- Why would the person have repressed the memory of the car accident?

REGRESSION

Regression happens when our mind retreats to behaviors from a younger time in life. It's like taking one step back to feel safe when things get too stressful. Freud first described this defense mechanism, where a person unconsciously goes back to an earlier developmental stage (Freud, 1953). For example, if someone is feeling overwhelmed at school, they might cling to a blanket or favorite toy—just like when they were very young.

Kids often regress during big life changes. A child who has stopped wetting the bed might start again after a new sibling is born—that change can feel too big, so their brain asks for the comfort of earlier times (Freud, 1963). Adults do this too. Imagine someone having a big fight with a coworker, and they throw a temper tantrum. That behavior reflects regression—acting like a child to deal with stress.

Regressing is not always bad—it is often a way to get temporary comfort. An older person facing death may start calling for their parent or act dependent again because deep worries feel better handled in a familiar, childlike way (Tatro & Marshall, 1982). But while regression offers short-term relief, it doesn't solve the real problem, and if used too often, it can get in the way of growing up emotionally.

Regression is like your brain saying, "I'm not okay right now," and handing the controls back to the lizard brain (Troncale, 2014). When something feels too stressful—like a fight, a big test, or losing someone you love—your mind may go back to a time when you felt safe: childhood. That's why a stressed-out adult might throw a tantrum, or a child might act like a baby when a new sibling is born. These behaviors aren't planned—they're automatic reactions from the lizard brain. It's trying to protect you by sending you back to a time that felt more comforting and less threatening. So even though the person may look silly or immature, regression is actually the lizard brain stepping in and saying, "Let me handle this. I've done it before."

In contrast to the lizard brain, the wizard brain helps us understand our feelings and gives us tools to cope better. When you realize you're regressing (or see it in someone else), the wizard brain can help you pause, breathe, and find a more helpful way to deal with stress—like talking it out, asking for help, or using grounding exercises. When we practice self-awareness and emotional regulation, we train our wizard brain to stay in charge more often—even when life gets hard.

Recently I have had several college students (seniors) come to class for their final course presentations dressed in Spongebob Squarepants pajamas and slippers, looking disheveled, and in tears. Despite having discussed the final project and presentation for many weeks in class, they appeared not only scared and unprepared, but reverted to behaviors of children. I can understand that anyone might be anxious giving a presentation, but there are many ways to experience and express anxiety. Over my many years of teaching, I have never seen such obvious examples of regression. These students might have relied more on their wizard brain instead of their lizard brains. Perhaps when we had discussed the project in the previous weeks of the course, they could have followed my suggestions to make a timeline, map out tasks, and create smaller deadlines for themselves. In addition, they could have made an appointment with me to discuss their concerns ahead of time.

Scenario Exercise

Imagine you are an employee in a busy office. You've been juggling multiple projects, dealing with tight deadlines, and trying to manage the expectations of your boss. It's been a particularly challenging week, and you're feeling overwhelmed. You have just received some critical feedback from your manager, and instead of feeling motivated to improve, you experience a rush of anxiety and frustration.

Instructions
Part 1: Identifying Regression

Read the scenario carefully. Then, read the different possible responses of regression to this stressful situation.

Responses:
1. **You find yourself crying uncontrollably in the bathroom.**
   You feel overwhelmed by the feedback and can't stop crying, just like you did as a child when things felt too difficult to handle.

2. **You binge-watch cartoons or childhood TV shows to avoid thinking about work.**
   You retreat to an activity you enjoyed as a child, allowing yourself to escape into a simpler, carefree time.
3. **You avoid going to work for a day, pretending to be sick.**
   You lie about being unwell to avoid facing the challenging work situation, seeking comfort in the avoidance of responsibility.

Part 2: Reflection

Now that you've analyzed the possible responses, reflect on the following questions:

1. *Why is* each of the responses a form of regression?
   (Consider behaviors that might indicate a return to an earlier developmental stage when you felt safer or more protected.)
2. What need might each regressive behavior be attempting to fulfill?
   (For example, seeking comfort, escaping anxiety, or avoiding responsibility.)
3. In each scenario, what would be a healthier or more mature way to cope with the stress?
   (Consider responses like talking to a mentor, taking a break to calm down, or using mindfulness techniques.)

ANGER

Anger is an obvious "fight" form of defensiveness (Rodriguez Mosquera et al., 2008). One study described anger as "designed to bargain for better treatment" (Sznycer et al., 2022). Outrage at injustice or mistreatment is common. Anger is a powerful emotion that clearly aims to protect, sometimes hiding other more vulnerable feelings underneath it such as sadness or fear (Hendel, 2018).

The anger may be directed toward a specific issue you feel strongly about, such as child abuse, or one may experience generalized anger at learning about injustices in institutions and social systems. Anger is necessary as a part of social change, but to be truly effective, it must be directed toward helpful and productive outlets. For example, if you are angry after seeing a documentary about the slaughter of gorillas in the wild, or the inhuman treatment of animals in game parks, a constructive channeling of that anger could be to invest time and money into education regarding these tragic practices. Consider alternative ways of conserving wildlife that may be critically endangered.

Thinking about diversity and inclusion can make people mad. Perhaps this workbook has already triggered your anger. It makes sense to feel angry, which is often a protection against threat (Dottolo, 2019). Sometimes we feel more powerful when we are angry, and for men, it might be the only emotion they are allowed to express.

Rhode Island is the most Catholic state in the nation (Goodnough, 2012). A local public high school displayed a large religious prayer in its auditorium. In 2012, a federal judge ruled that the prayer was unconstitutional, violating the principle of religious neutrality in government. Jessica Ahlquist, a 16-year-old student at that high school, initiated the case. In response, the community overwhelmed her with threats of violence, necessitating that the police escort her to school. The community was angry at the student's request to remove the prayer from the public school. In this instance, they acted out against her.

Counterattack involves expressing anger as a form of defense; an attack in response to a perceived threat or attack (Miller & Josephs, 2009). It is often a result of "either/or" thinking, as if there are only two options or ways of thinking. It is a quick response that does not take into consideration the other side. For example, when learning that convicted sex offenders are more likely to be White, middle-class, and married men (Corrigan, 2006), someone might respond, "not my husband!" In this instance, the person perceived this information as threatening, as an attack on *all* White, middle-class, married men, and defended against this with a counterattack.

Another example is often seen in conversations around police brutality, where someone might say, "but my dad is a cop!" or "not all police officers are bad." What is important to understand here is that most discussions around police brutality as a topic of concern are not centered on every and all police officers. Police brutality is about a system, a culture, of law enforcement as well as ideas about criminality and justice that end up being enacted upon individuals. *Some* police officers engage in that unjust violence, while many do not. However, this should not prohibit the discussion of the pattern of police brutality.

Once a colleague told me that she was worried about her white son, a college student in a fraternity. She was concerned that when he wore his fraternity sweatshirt to the first day of class, that his professor would see him as a "white guy in a fraternity." I responded, "but isn't he?" She became furious, outraged that I had, in her words, "attacked her son." She never spoke to me again. This example illustrates how anger, especially counter-attack, can function as a defense against a perceived threat. The colleague was likely sensitive and uncomfortable about her son's role in a fraternity, and she may have understood my response as an indictment of her son, which it was not.

Exercise

Can you notice points in this workbook that made you mad? What were they? Why did they make you mad? Did you have moments of counterattack?

Outside of this workbook, in your life, what really makes you angry? Perhaps it is an argument you had with someone recently, or a specific topic.

Think more closely about that anger. Think about your emotions as different parts of yourself, or different characters that live inside you, as in the Disney film "*Inside Out*" (2015). Imagine you could take away the anger for a moment and put it aside, acknowledging that it is important and useful. Now, what's underneath the anger? What is anger helping to protect you from?

PROTECTIVENESS OF OTHERS

Protectiveness of others is guarding someone else from a perceived attack. When encountering the previously mentioned fact about convicted sex offenders who are more likely to be heterosexual, white men (Corrigan, 2006), a woman might turn to one of the men nearby and assure him, "that doesn't mean you!" Again, the information was perceived by the woman as a threat (perhaps to all men), and as women are especially socialized as caretakers (Sharma et al., 2016) and peacemakers, they sometimes want to come to the rescue, feeling defensive when they believe someone else is being attacked. The man sitting nearby may not have interpreted the information as a threat at all, understanding that it did not apply to him. The woman "misheard" the information as applying to all heterosexual white men. This seems threatening to her, as it makes her consider all the straight, white men in her life. Of course, the statistic is *not* about all straight, white men, but instead about convicted sex offenders. However, the woman's sensitivity and perception is what inspired her need to "protect" the man, but she is really protecting her own relationships with heterosexual, white men.

This form of defensiveness is a demonstration of externalization (Gibson, 2015). In the previous example, the woman perceives the "bear" or the "dangerous" information, and she moves it outside herself by running to the "rescue" of the man who is "attacked." In order to assuage her own anxiety, she turns to "fight" mode by soothing what she thinks is the man's injury. This likely happens outside of her awareness, under the surface of consciousness (Freud, 1923).

Protectiveness of others also serves to maintain the status quo, making sure systems of power stay in place. A common reaction to learning about statistics that women are often victims of rape and sexual violence (Kilpatrick et al., 1998), sometimes people respond with, "but men are raped too!" Sometimes this protectiveness can look like competing victimization, as if there is a contest in suffering or oppression. Of course, we know that men and boys are victims of sexual assault and that there are gender differences in reporting (Pino & Meier, 1999). However, this shifts the focus from the topic at hand, which occurs at far greater rates, in order to redirect our attention (and anxiety) to another issue. We certainly need more research and understanding of all forms of violence against all groups of people. Nonetheless, when we shift our attention in this way, we avoid having to contend with the larger social structures of rape culture.

Remember that identifying defensiveness can help us become more emotionally intelligent. Refining our understanding of the ways our minds protect ourselves, getting specific, distinguishing one form from another, allows us to develop emotional granularity (McCoy, 2024). Remember that emotional granularity is when we can understand our feelings with nuance and specificity, like grains of sand. We are able to distinguish between emotions like fear and sadness, or the difference between anger and frustration. Growing our vocabulary for how we respond to threats can facilitate how we tend to our own needs and the needs of others. In our open-hearted state (Hendel, 2018), we can be more productive communicators.

Exercise

For this exercise, list as many words and phrases as you can in response to each question.

1. Answer this question: **What does it mean to be a "good man"?**
   Points to consider: What qualities do the men *you* respect and admire have? What values and morals do they live by? What kinds of things do they say and do?

2. Next, answer this question: **What does it mean to be a "real man"?**
   What do people mean when they say "be a man" or "man up"? What qualities are "real men" assumed to have? How are they expected to speak and act? How are they not supposed to behave?

3. What do you notice about the two lists? What are the similarities and differences between the words and phrases in each list? Are what it means to be a "good" man and a "real" man mostly similar or mostly different? Why do you think this is?
   How do you think these cultural messages affect boys and men? How might they affect girls and women?
   What feelings do you notice in yourself when you compare the two lists?

Sometimes people can feel defensive, especially *protective*, when the two lists are not the same. Sometimes the differences in the list are stark and can point out contradictions in our culture about expectations of men and boys. This can be illustrated in the idea that a "good man" is often described as thoughtful or caring, which is often not included in descriptors of what it means to be a "real man." Similarly, a "real man" is sometimes described as violent, tough, and stoic, which is not often on the list of what is considered a "good man."

When confronted with these conflicting ideas about manhood, people can react with protectiveness. It can be difficult to consider that men and masculinized people must choose between being a "good man" and a "real man." This choice can be uncomfortable and scary. Similarly, women and feminized people can feel protective of their ideas about the men in their life, categorizing them as "real men" or "good men." This kind of choice between only two options can elicit feelings of being trapped, and, therefore, anyone might react in a protective way. Or, you might consider that your father is both a "good man" and a "real man." However, the qualities that you can name about your father in either or both categories might make you feel protective. You might also be protecting the "family order" and the "way things were" in your house.

DISPLACEMENT

Displacement is redirecting a negative emotion or "taking it out on" someone or something else (Freud, 1894; Vaillant, 1992). For example, my boss reprimands me at work and I am angry about it, so I come home and kick the dog. In this case, I have displaced my anger at my boss onto the dog. We transfer our feelings such as anger or frustration away from the original source onto a less-threatening target. After receiving a low grade on an exam, Phil slams the door as he leaves the classroom.

Displacement is sometimes confused with projection. This confusion is understandable because both forms of defensiveness involve rerouting our feelings away from ourselves. Displacement involves redirecting or transposing your negative feeling onto a different target, while projection is the accusation that someone else is feeling the way you do. In the aforementioned example, projection might occur if Phil accused his roommate of failing a math test. He might say, "Hey! I heard you failed your math test!" Phil would be redirecting his own feelings onto his roommate. However, the aforementioned example is displacement because, instead, Phil slams the door.

When I have an important meeting to attend, sometimes I displace my anxiety about the meeting onto my clothing, paying extra attention to what I wear. I might get especially stressed about which earrings or socks to match with my outfit, as though my clothing matters much more than it does. In this example, I displace my anxiety about the meeting onto my clothes.

This form of defensiveness serves to protect us because at some unconscious level, we understand that confronting the source of our feelings would be dangerous (Freud, 1923). Instead, we put them onto another person or object. This allows the systems to function as usual, maintaining the status quo. Since Phil cannot attack his professor, he slams the door instead. But it also prevents him from addressing the problem. Perhaps Phil could arrange a meeting with his professor to discuss the exam. First, he would need to acknowledge his anger and its source. Is Phil mad at the professor, or himself for not preparing for the exam? If Phil can move to a more open-hearted state

(Hendel, 2018), he might invoke some of the 8 Cs: calmness, curiosity, clarity, compassion, confidence, courage, creativity and connectedness (Schwartz & Sweezy, 2020). Then perhaps Phil could approach the professor with curiosity, with a list of questions, to learn more about what went wrong on the exam and how he could do better in the future.

Exercise: The Traffic Jam

Description: Lisa is stuck in heavy traffic on her way to an important meeting. She feels stressed and anxious about being late. She starts to yell at the driver in front of her for what she perceives as bad driving.

Questions:
- What is Lisa's original emotion or impulse?
- Who or what is she directing her anger toward instead?
- How could Lisa manage her stress in a more constructive manner?
- How might displacement affect relationships and mental health in the long term?
- Can you think of a personal experience where you may have used displacement? How did it affect you or others?

REACTION FORMATION

Reaction formation is expressing the opposite of what one truly feels (Freud, 1923). This psychological defense mechanism was first introduced by Sigmund Freud. It involves the unconscious conversion of unwanted or anxiety-provoking impulses into their opposites, often in an exaggerated or extreme form. This defense mechanism serves as a way for individuals to protect themselves from feelings or thoughts that they find intolerable, by suppressing them and expressing behaviors that are diametrically opposed. As with many of the other forms of defensiveness, reaction formation is an unconscious process where the individual is unaware of using it, occurring far beneath the iceberg of awareness.

A common example of reaction formation is when a person feels anger and resentment toward a parent. As a child, this may have been especially dangerous to harbor such feelings about the person they depended upon for survival. Instead, the person proclaims that they had the "best mom in the world" in an exaggerated or unrealistic fashion. They might make claims such as, "my mom was never angry," or "my mom never made a mistake." The threat of considering negative feelings about their mother is too scary, so they turn the experience into its opposite. Or, for example, if someone feels jealousy or competitiveness towards a coworker for getting a promotion, they may go out of their way to compliment them or act excessively supportive, all while suppressing their true feelings of resentment. The feelings of jealousy are uncomfortable (the "angry bear"), so the person unconsciously transforms them into their more tolerable and "nicer" opposite.

A parent who had an emotionally distant or neglectful upbringing may, as an adult, overly indulge their children with affection, attention, and material gifts, trying to provide the opposite of the neglect they experienced. They may be so excessive in their affection that it becomes problematic, as they may be overcompensating for their own emotional deprivation. The important point here is that the behavior is exaggerated, causes problems, and is unrealistic or problematic. Someone who harbors homophobic tendencies might become excessively involved in advocacy for LGBTQ+ rights. While their internal feelings may be rooted in fear or discomfort, they exhibit behavior contrary to their true beliefs in an attempt to mask these internal contradictions. A person who feels guilty about their own sexual desires may become overly moralistic or preach excessively about chastity. The extreme moral stance becomes a reaction formation to their repressed sexual urges. By condemning the behavior in others, they can avoid confronting their own internal conflicts. Freud's daughter, Anna Freud (1918), explains that reaction formation serves as a way to protect the individual from anxiety associated with their repressed drives and wishes, turning what would be shameful or unacceptable impulses into behaviors that align with societal norms.

Exercise

Instructions: What follows are three scenarios. Read each and determine:
- What the person's **true feelings** or impulses might be.
- **How** reaction formation is playing a role.
- The potential **consequences** of this behavior.

Scenarios

1. Anna secretly feels jealous of her best friend's success. Instead of expressing jealousy, she showers her friend with constant praise and gifts, even when unnecessary.
2. Mark grew up in a household with lenient rules and secretly resented the lack of discipline. As an adult, he is an extremely strict parent, enforcing rigid rules even in situations where flexibility would be reasonable.
3. A teacher who struggled in school as a child now ridicules students who struggle with their studies, emphasizing strict discipline rather than empathy.

Now Reflect

- Have you ever exaggerated a behavior or belief to hide the opposite feeling?
- Think of a time when someone you knew seemed to overcompensate in their behavior. What do you think their hidden feelings were?
- What strategies can you use to be more aware of your true emotions rather than suppressing them?

UNDOING

You can think about undoing as an extension of reaction formation. If reaction formation is changing a feeling into its opposite, undoing is where a person tries to negate or "cancel out" an unacceptable thought, feeling, or action by engaging in behaviors that symbolically compensate for or reverse it. This mechanism helps reduce guilt, anxiety, or internal conflict caused by the original thought or action (Vaillant, 1992). Originally described by Sigmund Freud (1926), undoing operates at an unconscious level and often appears in rituals, compulsive behaviors, or exaggerated attempts to make amends.

For instance, a person who unintentionally insults a friend may later shower them with excessive compliments or gifts to "undo" the perceived damage. A superstitious individual might knock on wood or perform a small ritual after having a negative thought, believing it will prevent something bad from happening. Someone who cheats on their partner may suddenly start buying expensive gifts, planning romantic getaways, or becoming overly affectionate to subconsciously "erase" their guilt. A person who engages in a dishonest act, such as lying or stealing, might feel compelled to excessively clean their surroundings, symbolically "washing away" their guilt. Someone who feels guilty for being rude in an argument may apologize repeatedly and go out of their way to be overly nice, even if the other person has already forgiven them. A student who performed poorly on one test may study excessively for the next one, not just to improve but to symbolically "erase" the previous failure.

In cases of abuse, *undoing* can be part of a harmful cycle that prevents true accountability and change (Wilson, 2006). Recognizing this pattern is essential for breaking free from it. True healing requires honest acknowledgment of harm, real behavioral change, and often external support. If you or someone you know is experiencing domestic violence, consider seeking help from a trusted friend, counselor, or a domestic violence support organization.

As a way to respond to the "angry bear," undoing can function as a form of emotion regulation, to make the "bad" feelings go away (Cramer, 2000). While it can provide temporary relief, relying on undoing excessively can prevent individuals from addressing the root cause of their emotions. Recognizing this behavior can help in developing healthier coping strategies.

Exercise

Sakiko is a school principal and has been feeling stressed due to tight deadlines. One afternoon, during a meeting, she unintentionally dismisses a colleague's idea in a frustrated tone. After the meeting, Sakiko realizes that she may have come across as rude and starts feeling guilty.

Instead of addressing it directly, Sakiko spends the next few days overly praising that colleague in meetings, bringing them coffee, and offering to help with their tasks—even ones that are not her responsibility. Despite her efforts, she still feels anxious, worrying that her colleague might secretly be upset. The colleague, meanwhile, appreciates Sakiko's kindness but finds her behavior confusing and wonders why she is acting differently.

- What behaviors in this scenario show that Sakiko is using *undoing* as a defense mechanism?
- What emotions is she trying to avoid or compensate for?
- How might Sakiko's actions affect her relationship with her colleague?

- Does her behavior actually resolve the issue, or does it create more confusion?
- What could Sakiko have done instead of relying on *undoing*?
- Have you ever tried to "undo" a mistake instead of addressing it directly?
- How did it affect your feelings and the situation overall?
- How can you remind yourself to face uncomfortable emotions instead of overcompensating for them?

DISTANCING

Distancing involves separating or creating space between the self and the injustices of society (Spivey, 2005). This is most evident when people talk about how "society" is unjust or that "society" is "going to hell in a handbasket." When we hear about the opioid crisis, sometimes people react by mentioning how "society is just terrible nowadays." This serves to communicate the idea that "society" is *way over there*, separate from the speaker, that they are not part of it at all.

Another way that distancing is demonstrated is in comments such as, "My wife is Latina, so I can't be racist." The speaker is trying to put distance between themselves and racist beliefs, while also creating distance between themselves and "bad" white people. Sometimes this is in an attempt to legitimate themselves as a "good white" person. This is classically articulated in the statement, "some of my best friends are Black." In creating closeness with people who are oppressed, it sometimes functions as an attempt to distance us from those with power, even though we are a member of the more dominant group.

We need to remember that *we* are "society"; that we have learned the values, messages, and ideologies of "society"; and that many of those ideas have been internalized by us. Distancing provides protection from those uncomfortable or painful realizations and also serves to increase our hostility toward others. Sometimes someone might say, "look, my son is gay, so I'm not homophobic," and then follow this comment with a homophobic remark. The first part of the comment is intended to legitimate and distance the speaker from the harm.

In creating space between ourselves and systemic injustice, we avoid having to think about how we participate in, or benefit from, those systems. We fend off any guilt or shame that might arise, allowing us to escape responsibility. Remember the change triangle (Hendel, 2018) tells us that we want to protect ourselves from those negative emotions. We can see this defense as a response to *cognitive dissonance*, or the discomfort of holding two contradictory beliefs at the same time (Aronson, 1969). When hearing about a recent hate crime where a gay man was murdered, a parent of a gay man may be contending with their fear and worry for their son, while also questioning how they may have participated in their son's suffering about his sexuality growing up. In order to avoid this discomfort, the parent might say "look, my son is gay, so I'm not homophobic." The parent is negotiating two conflicting ideas or feelings. The first is their fear and worry about their son's safety. The second may be their guilt as they recall using homophobic language around their son when he was growing up or initially rejecting the idea that their son was gay.

Exercise

Can you think of some examples you have seen in the media of distancing? Maybe it was from a politician, or a legislator. Maybe it was on a sitcom or reality show. Describe the context and how you saw distancing in action.

Exercise

Think about a recent conversation or situation where you might have used **psychological distancing**, either consciously or unconsciously. Consider how you might have distanced yourself from personal accountability by focusing on broader societal issues or referencing your identity in a way that shut down a more personal conversation.

Reflect on how distancing might affect your relationships and how you might shift toward deeper engagement in the future.

1. **Identifying the Distance**
    - Was there a recent moment when you avoided addressing a personal issue by shifting the conversation to broader societal concerns (e.g., talking about systemic injustice, the state of the world, or referencing your identity)?

- How did you feel about the larger issues you brought up in that moment? Were you genuinely concerned or were you using them as a way to avoid the conversation?
- What was the emotional tone of the conversation when you distanced yourself? Did you feel a sense of relief, avoidance, or discomfort afterward?

2. **The Use of Identity in Deflection**
    - Reflecting on the phrase "My wife is Latina, so I can't be racist" or "Some of my best friends are Black," how might you have used similar statements in past conversations to distance yourself from accusations or uncomfortable topics?
    - Did you use your identity (e.g., being an ally, having diverse friends, or being connected to marginalized groups) to create emotional distance in that situation? How did it affect the conversation?
    - How do these types of identity-based comments work to protect you from feeling vulnerable or being seen as part of the problem?

3. **Impact on the Relationship**
    - How do you think the other person felt when the conversation shifted from the personal issue to societal concerns? Did they feel heard, dismissed, or disconnected from you?
    - What role did emotional withdrawal (checking your phone, leaning away, or avoiding eye contact) play in the conversation? How did this affect the other person's ability to engage or express their feelings?

4. **Understanding the Underlying Fear or Discomfort**
    - What might have been the underlying reason for your desire to distance yourself from the personal issue? Were you avoiding difficult emotions (e.g., guilt, shame, fear of conflict)? Can you connect these to the change triangle (Hendel, 2018)?
    - How do societal issues or your identity as a member of a dominant group make it easier to deflect responsibility in personal relationships?

5. **Engaging with Vulnerability**
    - How can you shift from psychological distancing to engaging more authentically in personal conversations? What would it look like to sit with the discomfort of the situation rather than deflecting it?

6. **Action Steps for Growth**
    - How can you become more aware of when you're using psychological distancing in conversations, especially around issues of personal responsibility or uncomfortable emotions?
    - What specific steps can you take in future conversations to stay more present and accountable, even when the larger societal context may feel overwhelming or distracting?

Reflection on Change:
- After completing this exercise, what insights have you gained about your communication style and use of psychological distancing? What might you try to do differently next time?

RELIGIOUS OR BIOLOGICAL LAW

Some people use religious or biological law to justify inequalities. For example, using the Bible, Torah, and/or Koran to explain why a group of people should be oppressed or deemed to be unacceptable by the culture is a demonstration of this defense mechanism. Another example is when religious scholars "discover" biological differences between groups to support a religious script. Nineteenth-century scholars spent a great deal of energy "proving" that women were less intelligent than men were on the basis of brain size and shape (Shields, 1975). These claims were used to justify excluding women from education, entering the workforce, voting, and participating in a variety of other fields. This cannot be discounted as having occurred "a long time ago" and would not happen today. Actually, the field of evolutionary psychology is growing (Chrisler, 2007) and scholars are still searching for brain-based differences (Brizendine, 2006), hormonal influences (Berenbaum & Beltz, 2016), and searching for the "gay gene" (Hamer, 2011).

The idea is not that religion or biology should be abandoned, but when they are used as weapons to justify why some people should have certain rights, or access to resources, then it is being used as a defense. The subjugation of women and the required submissiveness to male authority can be found in religious texts. Women are frequently cast as inferior, dependent on male domination reflecting the culture of the ancient times in which these texts were written. Conservative Christians and fundamentalists of various religions often cling to these narratives to determine the continued lower status of women (Nicholson & Domoney-Lyttle, 2020).

Historically, supporters of slavery cited the Biblical scriptures. They used the passage in Ephesians 6:5-9 which reads, "Slaves, obey our earthly master with respect and trembling" along with Timothy 6:1-2 that tells those who are slaves to regard their masters "as worthy of all honor." Even though race is not mentioned in the Bible, passages such as these were interpreted to legitimize racialized slavery (Haynes, 2002; Whitford, 2017).

Exercise

Instructions

Think about a time when you used or heard someone use religious principles or biological laws (e.g., "This is just how God intended," "Men and women are biologically different, that's just how it is," "The Bible says...") as a way to justify or deflect a personal issue or emotional discomfort. Reflect on how these arguments might have been used as a shield to avoid engaging in deeper, more vulnerable conversations.

1. **Identifying the Use of Religious or Biological Law**
   - Can you recall a situation where religious principles or biological arguments were used to shut down a conversation or avoid personal responsibility? What was the issue at hand?
   - What specific religious or biological argument was used to distance the speaker from the issue? How was it framed (e.g., "God says X," "Biologically, men/women are meant to do Y")?

2. **Motivations Behind the Defense Mechanism**
   - Why do you think the person (or you) used religious or biological law to avoid addressing the situation? What emotional or personal discomfort were they (or you) trying to avoid?
   - Did you feel that the religious or biological argument provided a sense of certainty or control in an otherwise uncertain or emotionally charged situation?
   - Were these laws invoked to show moral superiority or to distance oneself from the "problem"? If so, how did it serve to separate the speaker from others or from a difficult issue?

3. **Impact on the Conversation and Relationship**
    - How did the use of religious or biological laws affect the flow of the conversation? Did it shut down further discussion, create space for reflection, or distance the speaker emotionally from the other person involved?
    - How did the person on the receiving end of this argument (e.g., you, a friend, a colleague) feel? Did they feel dismissed, unheard, or frustrated by the defense mechanism?
4. **Examining the Underlying Beliefs**
    - When religious or biological laws are used in this way, what underlying belief or value might be at play? Is there a desire to be seen as morally right, to avoid blame, or to uphold a particular worldview?

Reframing the Conversation

- In hindsight, how could you or the other person have engaged with the conversation without resorting to a religious or biological defense? What other ways could you have addressed the emotional complexity or the personal responsibility at hand?
- Imagine that, instead of using religious or biological laws as a defense, you chose to stay present and engage more authentically with the difficult emotions or conflicts. How might that have changed the conversation or your relationship?
- What are some phrases or strategies you could use in future conversations to engage with difficult issues without defaulting to deflection through religious or biological laws?

Reflecting on the Growth of Compassionate Communication

- After completing this exercise, do you feel more aware of how religious or biological arguments might be used to distance yourself from emotionally challenging conversations?
- How can embracing the human complexity of situations—rather than reducing them to absolute rules—help you engage in more compassionate and relational communication in the future? What changes

do you want to make in your communication style to create more openness, emotional intimacy, and responsibility in your relationships? How does this exercise make you think about the open heartedness in the change triangle (Hendel, 2018)?

SUBLIMATION

Sublimation is a defense mechanism in which socially unacceptable impulses or desires are transformed into socially acceptable, often productive, behaviors. Originating from Sigmund Freud's psychoanalytic theory, sublimation is viewed as one of the most adaptive and constructive defenses, allowing individuals to channel potentially disruptive drives (e.g., aggression, sexuality) into outlets that contribute to society (Freud, 1953). Unlike repression or denial, which simply suppress impulses, sublimation redirects them in a way that maintains inner equilibrium without social or personal harm.

In his studies of ego defenses, Vaillant (1992) placed sublimation at the top of his hierarchy of defense mechanisms due to its adaptive and prosocial qualities. He found in longitudinal research that individuals who used sublimation were more likely to enjoy psychological well-being, career success, and interpersonal stability. Sublimation is also associated with resilience, emotional intelligence, and strong ego functioning (Perry & Bond, 2012).

For example, a person who struggles with anger might channel this into martial arts, boxing, or intense physical exercise. An individual experiencing sexual tension might pour this energy into creating music, painting, or writing poetry. Someone with controlling tendencies may redirect this drive into organizing community initiatives or leading projects. These examples reflect how sublimation allows individuals to meet their emotional needs while conforming to cultural expectations.

Alex, a 17-year-old high school student, frequently feels intense frustration due to family conflict and pressure to succeed academically. Instead of acting out aggressively or withdrawing emotionally, Alex begins running long distances after school. Over time, this coping strategy evolves into participation in cross-country competitions. Running becomes not just an outlet for emotional tension but a source of personal pride and social recognition. Here, Alex unconsciously uses sublimation to channel emotional conflict into constructive behavior, enhancing both psychological and physical health.

Sublimation allows us to take the energy of dissonance—the guilt, fear, or anxiety that comes when we act outside our values—and transform it into purposeful action. Remember that cognitive dissonance is when we hold contradictory beliefs at the same time (Aronson, 1969). Rather than staying stuck in denial or rationalization (less healthy defenses), sublimation gives us a way to resolve the discomfort while also contributing positively to our lives and communities.

Reflective Exercise: Identifying Sublimations in Your Life

Use this guided journal prompt to explore your own sublimation processes:

Step 1: Awareness of Impulses

- Think of a strong emotion or impulse you've had recently that felt socially or personally uncomfortable (e.g., anger, jealousy, desire for revenge, etc.).
  Example: I felt intense irritation when a co-worker took credit for my work.

Step 2: Initial Response

- How did you respond to that emotion? Did you express it, suppress it, or channel it elsewhere?
  I went to the gym and lifted weights instead of confronting them directly.

Step 3: Assess the Outcome

- Was your action beneficial to your well-being or others? Did it help you process the emotion?
  Yes, I felt calmer afterward and was able to address the issue professionally later.

Step 4: Reframing

- Can you see this response as a form of sublimation? What insight does that offer you?
  I realized that physical activity is one of my healthiest outlets for emotional stress.

Reflection Prompt:

"How might I continue to develop ways of transforming difficult emotions into meaningful or creative actions?"

Sublimation exemplifies the human capacity to transform psychological discomfort into growth, creativity, and social contribution. Recognizing and cultivating sublimation can promote emotional regulation, deepen self-understanding, and foster adaptive behavior in both personal and professional settings.

COMPETING VICTIMIZATION

Competing victimization refers to a psychological and social phenomenon in which individuals or groups highlight their own suffering—real or perceived—as a way to deflect attention from others' pain, avoid accountability, or maintain a sense of moral superiority. While not traditionally labeled as a "classical" defense mechanism in psychoanalysis, it operates similarly to projection, denial, or moral disengagement by protecting the ego from guilt, shame, or discomfort (Bandura, 1999; Cramer, 2006). This kind of defense often happens when people have arguments, especially in politics or when talking about groups and fairness. Instead of admitting that someone else has been hurt, a person focuses on their own problems. They try to show that their pain is bigger or more important.

Researchers like Volkan (2004) and Staub (2006) have studied this idea in how groups of people act, especially after conflicts or fights. Sometimes, groups try to show they have been hurt the most to get sympathy or to justify getting back at others. This is called "competitive victimhood," where groups want to prove they suffered more so they can support their story or avoid blame for causing harm (Noor et al., 2008). It helps someone avoid feeling weak or upset by not admitting they might have caused harm. This way, the person can still see themselves as "good" or "innocent" and avoid feeling guilty, sorry, or responsible for what happened (Baumeister et al., 1994).

Example

INTERPERSONAL EXAMPLE

During a conversation about how his partner feels unsupported at home, Sam quickly responds, "Well, *I'm* the one working 50 hours a week, and no one's asking how *I* feel." While Sam may indeed be overworked and underappreciated, this redirection minimizes his partner's valid emotional experience. Instead of engaging in reflection or repair, Sam unconsciously seeks to restore his sense of self-worth through comparative suffering.

SOCIOPOLITICAL EXAMPLE

When discussions of racism arise, some individuals respond with, "Well, I've been poor and white my whole life, so don't tell me I have privilege." While economic hardship is real, this response derails the conversation about racial inequality by centering another form of suffering (social class), rather than engaging with the specific harm of racism (Applebaum, 2010).

Reflective Exercise: Recognizing Competing Victimization

Use the following exercise to identify and reflect on your own or others' use of competing victimization:

Step 1: Recall a Conflict Situation

Think of a time when someone brought up an issue about being hurt, overlooked, or mistreated—either personally or socially.

> *Example: A friend shared how they felt dismissed during a team project.*

Step 2: Notice Your Internal Response

What was your first impulse—did you feel defensive, invalidated, or eager to express your own grievance?

> *I immediately wanted to say how stressed I was and how I felt no one helped me either.*

Step 3: Examine the Motivation

Ask: Was I trying to genuinely share, or was I unconsciously shifting focus to protect myself from feeling guilt, inadequacy, or blame?

> *Maybe I didn't want to admit I dropped the ball and felt ashamed.*

Step 4: Reframe and Practice Empathy

Challenge yourself: What would it feel like to validate the other person's pain first, before discussing your own?

> *I could have said, "You're right, I should've supported you more. Tell me how that felt."*

Journal Prompt

> *"When do I feel most tempted to highlight my own suffering during a difficult conversation? What feelings am I avoiding in those moments, and how might I approach them with more empathy and openness?"*

Competing victimization may serve as a subtle, socially acceptable way to deflect accountability and maintain self-esteem, but it often prevents genuine connection and healing—both in personal relationships and across cultural or political divides. Awareness of this defense can create space for humility, dialogue, and ultimately, growth.

INTELLECTUALIZATION

Intellectualization occurs when, instead of facing strong emotions like sadness, fear, or anger, a person might focus only on the facts or ideas about the situation. They use thinking instead of feeling to protect themselves. It's like putting a wall of logic between yourself and your emotions. For example, someone whose pet dies might talk about how pet lifespans work or how animals are part of the food chain—but they avoid talking about how heartbroken they feel. This doesn't mean they don't care. It means they're using intellectualization to avoid the pain that comes with loss. This is one way people try to stay emotionally safe during hard times (Cramer, 2006).

People often use intellectualization when their feelings are too big or scary to deal with right away. Talking about things in a smart or logical way can feel safer. This defense helps them stay calm and feel in control. Freud (1966) believed that people do this without even realizing it—it's an unconscious way to cope. While this can be helpful sometimes—like during an emergency when staying calm is important—it can also cause problems.

If someone never lets themselves feel their emotions, they might become disconnected from what's really going on inside. Over time, this can make relationships harder or cause stress to build up without a healthy way to let it out (Vaillant, 1992).

It's important to know that intellectualization is not the same as just being smart or curious. It becomes a defense mechanism when a person uses logic to avoid emotions, especially during times when it would be healthy to feel something. For example, a student who fails a test might start talking about how testing systems are flawed instead of admitting they feel disappointed or embarrassed. Perry and Bond (2012) explain that intellectualization can be helpful if it's balanced—used along with emotional awareness. But if it becomes the only way a person deals with hard things, it can stop them from growing emotionally or connecting with others in a real way.

If you notice yourself always explaining things without feeling anything, you might be using intellectualization too much. It can help to slow down and ask yourself: *What am I really feeling right now?* Learning to sit with emotions, even when they're uncomfortable, is an important part of growing up and building strong relationships.

Intellectualization is often associated with internalizing (Gibson, 2015) because it involves turning away from emotions and instead relying on cognition. The person doesn't lash out (externalizing), but contains or represses the emotional energy, often translating it into rational explanations, theories, or problem-solving strategies. For example, Chris loses a loved one but doesn't cry or talk about their feelings. Instead, they read several academic papers about the psychology of grief and explain the five stages of mourning to others. This is intellectualization, and it's an internalizing response because Chris is avoiding outward emotional expression and dealing with pain by thinking instead of feeling.

While intellectualization can offer short-term relief and make someone feel more "in control," over time, it may block emotional healing and lead to internalized distress like anxiety or somatic symptoms (Kirmayer & Looper, 1998). Psychologists emphasize that emotions need to be processed, not just explained. Otherwise, the emotional tension may show up later as physical problems or relationship issues.

Reflective Exercise: Not Just the Facts
Scenario
Samantha's friend moves to another city, and Samantha starts reading books about why people move and how it affects friendships. She tells her classmates it's "just part of life" and talks about statistics on moving. But she never says she's sad or misses her friend.

Activity
1. Write down what Samantha is *thinking* and what she might really be *feeling*.
2. Make two lists:
    - List 1: Things Samantha says out loud (logical facts)
    - List 2: Feelings Samantha might be hiding (emotions)

Reflection Prompts
- Have you ever acted like Samantha—focusing only on facts instead of feelings?
- What were you trying to avoid feeling?
- How might it help to talk about or express those feelings with someone you trust?
- What's one way you could balance your thoughts and emotions the next time something hard happens?

HUMOR

Humor isn't just about making people laugh. Sometimes, we use humor to protect ourselves from feeling hurt, scared, or embarrassed which is when humor is a defense mechanism. When people joke about a sad or stressful situation, they might be using humor to feel more in control or to hide how upset they really are. It's a way the brain helps us deal with big feelings without falling apart. According to Vaillant (1992), humor is one of the healthiest defense mechanisms. It helps people face difficult situations without being overwhelmed. Someone might joke about having a bad haircut instead of admitting they feel really embarrassed. Laughing can give us some space from our feelings until we're ready to deal with them.

Humor makes tough times feel easier. When people laugh together, they feel connected and less alone. During sad or scary moments, a funny comment can help everyone relax. This kind of humor isn't mean or used to hurt others—it's used to cope with feelings. In fact, researchers like Martin et al. (2003) found that people who use humor this way often feel less stress and bounce back from problems more quickly. However, it's important to know that not all humor is helpful. Sometimes people use jokes to avoid serious conversations or hide deep pain. If someone always makes jokes when things get emotional, it might mean they're having trouble facing their feelings (Cramer, 2006).

Humor can help someone talk about hard things in a softer way. For example, a student nervous about a big test might joke, "Hope my pencil knows the answers!" This makes others laugh, but it also shows the student is feeling anxious. That joke opens a door to talk about their feelings if they choose. Unhealthy humor, though, can hurt people or block emotions. If someone uses sarcasm or makes fun of others, that's not helpful—it's a way of pushing feelings away or avoiding being honest. Using humor in a kind, thoughtful way is a skill we can all learn. It's okay to laugh, but it's also okay to feel sad or scared. The key is balance.

Understanding how we use humor can help us build better friendships and take care of our emotions. If you notice you're always joking when things feel hard, it might be your brain's way of saying, "I need a break from these feelings." That's normal. But it's also helpful to check in with yourself and talk to someone you trust. Sometimes being honest—even just a little—can help more than a joke.

One way many marginalized people navigate the pain and mistreatment they received based on their race, class, gender, sexuality, disability, etc. is by using humor. Making jokes or laughing about a hard situation can help them feel stronger and more in control. Making jokes about serious topics—like racism or unfair laws—can help people speak out while also protecting their feelings. Outley et al. (2021) explain that humor can be used as a form of protest, letting people show how unfair something is without getting into a fight.

Even though humor can be helpful, it doesn't mean everything is okay. Sometimes, people joke so much that they don't get a chance to talk about how they really feel. A funny person might be hiding deep hurt. Ford and Ferguson (2004) studied how humor can help people feel better short-term, but it doesn't take away the pain if problems aren't solved. That's why it's important to listen when someone uses humor about serious topics—it might be a sign they're hurting inside.

Using humor doesn't mean someone is weak. In fact, it often takes a lot of strength and bravery. Many comedians from marginalized groups use jokes to tell the truth about their lives. They help people understand things like discrimination or poverty in a way that others can hear and think about. Martin et al. (2003) found that this kind of humor can build hope and bring people together. It's not just funny—it's powerful.

Reflective Exercise: Laughing It Off

Scenario

Jayla is the only girl on the robotics team. During meetings, some boys often interrupt her ideas or act like she doesn't know much. One day, when the teacher asks who came up with a great idea, the boys stay quiet—even though it was Jayla's idea.

Jayla jokes loudly, "Well, I guess I'm just invisible with superpowers!" Everyone laughs, and the moment moves on. But later, Jayla tells her best friend that the joke made her feel better because it stopped her from crying.

Reflection Questions

1. What was funny about what Jayla said?
2. How did humor help Jayla in that moment?
3. Do you think she was *only* joking, or do you think she was hiding a feeling?
4. Have you ever laughed about something that actually hurt you?
5. What's one kind thing someone could have said or done to support Jayla?

SUMMARY

In this chapter, we reviewed different ways that defensiveness might appear. Our unconscious mind has developed various forms of protecting us from threat. We explored multiple defense mechanisms, including denial, avoidance, minimization, rationalization, blaming the victim, projection, and anger, to name a few. Of course, this list is not exhaustive. Developing skills to better identify how defensiveness shows up can help us better understand underlying reasons and improve our relationships with ourselves and others. Now, let's turn our attention to some practical strategies for what to do in response to feelings of defensiveness.

Chapter 4
So Now What? What Can We Do?

*L*ark stays after class one day, waiting for the last student to trickle out. They are twisting the hem of their oversized denim jacket, clearly nervous.

"Dr. Felix," they begin, "can I ask you something kind of … weird?"

Dr. Felix smiles. "Try me."

"So, when we talk about intersectionality, I get it on paper. But like, in me, I don't know what parts I'm supposed to focus on. I'm queer. I'm nonbinary. I've also got anxiety and I'm autistic. And I'm white and middle-class. It's like … am I the oppressor or the oppressed? Or both?"

Dr. Felix's eyes soften. "Lark, that's not a weird question at all. That's *the* question. Intersectionality isn't about ranking oppression—it's about recognizing complexity. You contain multitudes. So does everyone in this room."

Lark exhales. "Okay. Cool. I just … I don't want to take up too much space, you know?"

Dr. Felix pauses. "If you're asking that question, you probably aren't."

Transforming Defensiveness: A Guidebook for Rewriting Our Stories & Reclaiming Connection, First Edition. Andrea L. Dottolo.
© 2026 John Wiley & Sons, Inc. All rights reserved, including rights for text and data mining and training of artificial intelligence technologies or similar technologies.
Published 2026 by John Wiley & Sons, Inc.

This chapter explores steps and practical strategies to address defensiveness. Often when learning about defensiveness, we find ourselves asking, "So now what? What can we *do*?"

In exploring possible ways to respond to defensiveness, the following discussion is organized into three topics, each with a different focus. The section titled "Focus on You" centers on tools and strategies to address your own experiences of defensiveness. This is the most important step, and in many ways, any other actions are not possible without first focusing on you. The section titled "Focus on Others" offers some ideas on how to address the defensiveness that happens in others, in our interpersonal relationships. As we will see, this is tricky since our defenses are established for a reason, and since they are mostly unconscious, you cannot "make" anyone see or respond to them. The section titled "Focus on Groups" proposes some suggestions for leaders, or those who manage groups where defensiveness arises. Some practical approaches to navigating conflict among others are discussed, especially for people in charge of group interactions, such as teachers, coaches, supervisors, administrators, or any other kind of leader.

FOCUS ON YOU

Let's begin by focusing on ourselves. First, our own thoughts, feelings, and behaviors are the only things we can control. What other people do isn't up to us at all. If we can understand ourselves, we can serve as models for people in our lives. When we have language and skills to navigate our own reactions, we can foster empathy with others, and perhaps even pass along some of our knowledge.

Let's start with the point that there is no single correct way to respond to defensiveness. Every interaction is different. You must make the best decision you can at the moment. Sometimes that means disengaging—you simply walk away. It might mean you stop and listen. Or, you might respond right then. Perhaps you might return to the topic much later, after you have had time to cool down and reflect.

The first most important step in recognizing your own defensiveness is awareness. First, we have to know defensiveness is present in order to move to a curious mindset. This can only be accomplished if we move away from our lizard brain and into our wizard brain (Hammond, 2014; Troncale, 2014).

Remember that the lizard brain activates the protective modes of fight, flight, freeze, or fawn. The lizard brain steals energy away from the wizard brain, which allows us to see clearly and respond thoughtfully. The wizard brain connects us to an open-hearted state (Hendel, 2018), or the 8 Cs (Schwartz & Sweezy, 2020). One of the 8 Cs that we will focus on here is *curiosity*. In shifting our attention away from needing to protect against threat to an intentional observation and awareness, we can learn. With curiosity, we can wonder, ask questions, pay attention, notice, and think more clearly. Without curiosity, we are stuck in old patterns of thoughts, feelings, and behaviors, which prohibit growth and change.

One way to think about applying this is with the BEAR method. Remember the BEAR? We have been discussing the source of threat as a large, angry bear from which our defenses protect us. Other scholars have used acronyms to succinctly describe a method of regulating our nervous systems (Brach, 2020; Purcell & Glinder, 2022). Let's return to the image we have been using throughout this book. Each letter of the word "bear" stands for a step in the process of recognizing defensiveness and hopefully moving to an open-hearted state (Hendel, 2018).

B = Breathe

E = Evaluate

A = Adjust

R = Respond

B represents **Breathe**. Stop. Notice that you feel something. When I first started learning about strategies such as these, instructors would often say, "Just breathe. Sit with it." I was left confused and frustrated at these directions. What does that mean? How am I supposed to do that? Sit with *what* exactly? Through more studying, I learned that there are some questions you can ask yourself that might be helpful. This is not an exhaustive list, and you do not have to engage with all of them, by any means. The questions are intended to guide you through this first step, which can sometimes be the most difficult since it begins with awareness.

You might consider: What are you feeling in your body? Pay attention to the tension. Can you breathe into that sensation, wherever it is? What is the quality of the sensation? Is it tight? Prickly? Burning? Fluttery? Does the sensation have a color? A shape? Texture? Smell? If the sensation could talk, what would it say? You might imagine a deflated balloon at the precise location of the tension (such as a knot in your shoulders) and envision that you could inhale into it, inflating the balloon completely. Take the biggest breath you have taken all day to fill the balloon with air. Then slowly exhale all of the air inside it until it is completely empty again (Brown & Gerbarg, 2012).

Try not to judge any part of the experience; just breathe. We know that breathing is the fastest way to regulate our nervous system (Levine, 1997; Purcell & Glinder, 2022; Van der Kolk, 2014). You might inhale slowly for a count of 4 and then exhale for a count of 4. Try to keep breathing through each step of the process.

It is important to mention that this step might be very challenging, especially for people with histories of trauma. Sometimes noticing the body can feel dangerous when the body has been the site of danger and/or violence (Herman, 2015; Levine, 1997; Van der Kolk, 2014). Thompson (1994) has argued that we need to critically examine our overuse of the term "body image," as that implies a picture that someone has in their mind's eye of their body. Many trauma survivors do not experience their body as connected to themselves, dissociating from the very place where they were betrayed. Instead, they might see themselves like a floating head, separated and removed from any part of the body. Thompson (1994) advocates that we use the term "body consciousness" instead, where an individual can cultivate an awareness of the relationship between that person and their body. As scary as it might seem to reconnect with the body and its associations with danger, the idea is to reestablish the breath and body as a safer space to land. Creating a new association between the body and feeling grounded and secure can take lots of work and patience. Consider seeing a licensed mental health counselor for assistance.

E stands for **Evaluate.** To evaluate is to assess, measure, appraise, examine, analyze. Take inventory. Collect some data about what is happening inside you. Try to notice and narrate what you identified while breathing. Evaluate your bodily sensations, trying to connect them to your emotions. Do you feel tightness in your chest? Is that fear? Excitement? Do you feel a burning sensation in your stomach? Are you angry? Frustrated? Is there a lump in your throat? Is that sadness? Is your feeling a reaction to the present moment, or something in your past? For example, a driver might cut me off in traffic and I get scared ... very scared. Feeling temporarily shocked or unnerved in such a situation might seem reasonable. However, if I am *extremely* frightened and find it difficult to recover, it could be that I am reminded of a car accident from many years ago. You might consider a scale of emotional intensity ranging from 1 (not strong) to 10 (very strong). If you notice your feeling is "beyond a 5," it means your emotion is high and could also indicate that your feeling is disproportionate to the situation at hand. Remember that naming our feelings is part of developing emotional intelligence.

A stands for **Adjust.** Adjust your perspective from your lizard brain to your wizard brain (Hammond, 2014; Troncale, 2014). You might consider that the letter **A** could also stand for **ask**, encouraging yourself to keep asking questions about your experience. Identify that defensiveness is operating for you. Recognize that your lizard brain took over there for a moment, but you can shift your consciousness by continuing to breathe. Your feeling is coming from a place, likely in response to a threat. You might consider which form of defensiveness is coming up for you. If you can't do that at this point, it's okay, since we often can't know exactly what is happening at the moment. However, if you try to stay calm and curious, you might be able to name what type of defense you are exhibiting.

R represents **Respond.** Notice the difference between the words "react" and "respond." Reacting is an automatic emotional response, like a reflex. Responding is a thoughtful, deliberate action that is intentional and mindful (Napoli, 2011; Smart & Segalowitz, 2017). While you are still breathing deeply, ask yourself what you would like to do next. Sometimes it can be helpful to remember that you have many options here. Defensiveness can sometimes arise when an individual feels trapped, so being reminded that we all have choices in any given moment can be useful. You might consider: What is the goal of the conversation? What is the best way to communicate to achieve your goal? Is this the best time? Should the conversation continue? If so, can I ease the fear? Can I change my tone of voice? Use different words or body language? Do I need to leave? Stop the conversation?

Transforming the threat of the "bear" into an acronym for a coping strategy can demonstrate that you have choices in your perception, interpretation, and application of your knowledge and skills. Remember that when you first learn a skill, you are a beginner. It will be difficult, and you will likely become frustrated. That's part of the process. The more you practice, the better you will get.

Shapiro (2012) describes what she calls the "Breathing Shift Technique." When you feel stress and disturbance in your body, notice your breathing. It is very common for the breath to feel like it is in the chest and throat, shallow, and quick. Shapiro (2012) instructs to place one hand on your chest, where the breathing is happening. Next, place your other hand over your lower stomach. This is where deeper, more relaxed breathing happens in the body. Now think about moving your breath, shifting its location lower in your abdomen, and slowing it down. Calming our physiology can be a first step in calming our minds.

If your defensiveness leads to behaviors you would like to change, consider a multipronged approach. You might seek counseling from a licensed professional such as a therapist. You might contact a life coach. You might read more books on the topic. Below is an exercise developed by Jeremy Sutton (2021) that asks pointed questions that might help you strategize about appropriate next steps for you (https://positive.b-cdn.net/wp-content/uploads/2021/08/What-Behavior-Do-I-Want-to-Change.pdf).

Exercise: What Behavior Do I Want to Change?

Poor behavior in the past often arises from unhelpful thinking habits, but that does not mean we have to continue with it into the future. Through reflecting on what has happened, our thinking, and our behavior, we can consider new responses and learn to react in a more positive, helpful way.

Use the questions below to provide the focus required to identify what behavior you would like to change and how this could be achieved.

- What is the behavior? (such as, arguing or yelling)
- What can I do to start preparing to change? (such as focusing on relaxation, taking time out when needed)
- What steps should I take to make this happen? (such as enrolling in a mindfulness class or taking some online training)
- What can other people do to help me change my behavior? (such as if you explain the changes you are trying to make, they could support you and remain patient)
- How will I know whether I am making progress? (such as ask a trusted friend to give you feedback)
- What should I do if I start to slip back to old habits? (such as keep a log of successes, review regularly, and see how the positive changes are helping)
- What can I do today to start these changes? (such as tell your close friend what you plan and how)

Changing how we think and react can take time, effort, and patience, yet the rewards make it worthwhile.

Similarly, the following exercise encourages you to map your responses, especially thoughts, emotions, behaviors, and physical sensations in order to understand the relationship between them (Sutton, 2021, Recognizing How We Think, Feel, and Behave). In doing so, you might take a closer look at how these interrelated elements of your psychology are connected. You can highlight and emphasize parts that are successful for you and also target areas for improvement.

Exercise: Recognizing How We Think, Feel, and Behave

Our mental and physical responses overlap and affect how we think, feel, and behave.

Creating a physical picture of how we respond—cognitively, emotionally, and physically—can help us understand why we behave as we do. Identifying patterns in our reactions and behavior can help us recognize opportunities to change unhelpful beliefs, thoughts, and automatic psychological processes.

Think of a difficult situation that you faced recently. Draw four circles on a piece of paper. Label the first circle "thoughts," the second "emotions," the third "behavior," and the fourth "physical sensations." Scribble or draw pictures beside each label to capture the impact of the event on each element. Draw lines or arrows between each of the categories and your responses to indicate that they are connected to one another.

Ask yourself:

- What can I learn from my thoughts, behavior, physical sensations, and emotions?
- Were they justified, rational, or appropriate?
- If not, what could I change?

One way to dissipate tension and negative energy is to move the body (Berger, 1994; Sharon-David & Tenenbaum, 2017). You might go for a walk, do yoga, run, or lift weights. You can also just engage in everyday movement such as walking the dog, doing household chores, taking the stairs, dancing, or parking farther away at the grocery store. Bodily movement not only helps with our physiology, but can also provide time and space away from a stressor (while requiring you to breathe) to get some perspective.

Focusing on you first is most important so that you can get a clearer picture of what you can control and what you cannot. Growth and change cannot happen without awareness first. Harro (2000) describes "waking up" and "getting ready" as the first two steps in the "cycle of liberation." She explains that understanding our histories and previous patterns of engagement become the foundation upon which we can then make active choices about how to move forward. These steps are followed by ones that involve others, including reaching out, building community, coalescing (joining together), and creating change (Harro, 2000). But you have to start with you.

Similarly, Robbins (2024) describes what she deems the "Let Them" theory. The premise is that when others trigger you, stress you out, or make you feel defensive, "let them." Step back and observe their behavior. Stop trying to control others and focus on yourself. Robbins (2024) continually reminds us that the *only* person you can control is yourself. When you can distinguish between what you can control and what you cannot, you reclaim power. The second part of the theory is "let me," which prioritizes *you*: your needs, wants, actions, feelings, possibilities. Robbins (2024) clarifies:

> *Let Them* is not an excuse to stop answering your phone, to shrug your shoulders, to refuse to talk it out with a friend or family member who is hurt, to stay in a situation that hurts you, or to ignore discrimination or dangerous people. It's not a license to give someone the silent treatment, ghost people, avoid hard conversations, or withdraw from your relationships.
>
> *(p. 49)*

Instead, we need to put ourselves first—stop trying to create an illusion of safety by attempting the impossible, which is to control another person. Sometimes when we feel defensive, we respond by arguing, yelling, pleading, begging, or any number of other behaviors to try to convince someone else that we are "right." It seems that the "Let Them" theory can work even more effectively once you have the language, tools, and skills to identify defensiveness in yourself and others. Once you can "see" and name what's happening, you can make the best decision for you. Again, that might mean taking a break, learning more, asking more questions, walking away, and checking your tone and body language. "Let them" and "let me" is a way to focus on you.

FOCUS ON OTHERS

Addressing defensiveness in others is very tricky, mostly because it is highly unsuccessful. As Robbins (2024) mentions, no one will change unless they really want to—this includes their thoughts, feelings, or behaviors. You can't "make" someone stop defending, especially when they are convinced of the threat of an "angry bear." You also can't "make" them implement the BEAR technique to get them to focus on themselves. However, there are many ways we can take direct action, always with the understanding that you may need to do so for you (and not them). You always need to assess your own physical and emotional safety in taking any kind of response.

Throughout this book, we have been investigating examples of the mistreatment of others in various ways, largely because they belong to a particular group. We have explored instances of racism, sexism, homophobia, ageism, Islamophobia, transphobia, and classism, to name a few. Discrimination has been applied on both individual and group levels so that one person might be targeted due to their group membership, or an entire collection of people are harmed or attacked. Many scholars have written about the ways that, at its core, oppression is rooted in fear (Allport, et al., 1954; David & Derthick, 2017; Young, 2008). It follows that prejudice and discrimination are forms of defensiveness, as a way to protect from the fear of threat. This fear applies to the individual bully on the playground (Lines, 2007), to small group divisions and cliques (Ellis & Zarbatany, 2017), and to widespread government policies that target a specific group (Higgs, 2006). Power holders scramble for control with abuse and force to cover up their internal feelings of fear and inferiority.

One powerful example of this occurred in Nazi Germany. After World War I, Germany was humiliated by its surrender, experiencing political, social, and economic loss (Scheff et al., 2018). As a way to manage fear and shame, Germany displaced blame onto the Jewish people (Scheff et al., 2018). This scapegoating can be seen as both displacement and blaming the victim, among others (Glick, 2005). By redirecting their attention onto a single group as a simple solution to a complex problem, Germans could unite against a "problem" and fight.

Sometimes encountering injustice in the forms of prejudice and discrimination can be interpreted as coming face-to-face with defensiveness. Furthermore, this can trigger our own defensiveness. If my cousin tells a racist joke at a family function as a result of his own unconscious feelings of fear, powerlessness, and inferiority, I might quickly feel defensive in response. When both of us are in our lizard brains, this again brings us out of our wizard brains (Barry & Welsh, 2007) and contrasts with an open-hearted state (Hendel, 2018) and the 8 Cs (DeMala-Moran, 2018). In discussing the defensiveness that occurs in our interpersonal relationships at home, work, and in the public domain, learners often ask: What can I do? What can I say?

Generally speaking, there are three factors that may influence whether someone might feel comfortable speaking up when witnessing discrimination:

power, relationships, and knowledge (Evans & Washington, 2010). For example, you might not feel safe confronting someone who wields power over you, like a police officer or your boss. Or, if you have more power over someone else, confronting prejudice might feel more possible. For example, if my little brother makes an insensitive comment, I might not hesitate to tell him to "knock it off."

It might feel quite different to speak up when you are directly targeted compared to when you witness someone else being mistreated because of their group membership. If someone is the only Muslim person in a room where Islamophobia is happening, it might be too dangerous to do anything. However, if a White and/or Christian person is in that room where Islamophobia is happening, it might be easier for them to directly question the others regarding their offensive remarks. The White/Christian in the aforementioned situation is acting as an ally to the Muslim community. Allies are "members of dominant social groups (e.g., men, Whites, heterosexuals) who are working to end the system of oppression that gives them greater privilege and power based on their social group membership" (Evans & Washington, 2010, p. 413).

Relationships can be an obstacle in speaking up when you don't want to "cause trouble" or pay a price for a confrontation. If my uncle insults my aunt at Thanksgiving, my mother might be mad at me for interfering, so I stay quiet. Or, if my relationship with my coworker is strong, built upon trust and communication, then I might feel safer broaching a difficult conversation, knowing that our relationship will withstand bumps in the road.

Knowledge can become an impediment to our ability to speak up on behalf of ourselves or someone else, especially when we "don't know what to say." When we confront mistreatment, we can feel stunned or trapped in our reaction. It is my hope that the content of this guidebook will help you build your vocabulary of words, skills, and strategies. In doing so, you become equipped with knowledge to speak your truth.

In focusing on the behavior of others, consider multiple options. Perhaps you cannot just sit back while someone tells a racist joke. One strategy is to simply not laugh. This alone can sometimes shift the energy in a conversation. Or, you might say, "that's not funny," or "that's not cool." Another idea is to ask the person to repeat themselves, or ask, "can you say that again?" Alternatively, you might act like you do not understand the joke, saying, "gee, I don't get it," so that the offender might have to articulate the statement more explicitly.

Applewhite (2019) encourages us to confront ageism when we see it, name it, and make the bias explicit. She suggests pointing out ageist beliefs and hypocrisies to your peers, especially if you are older. For example, when you see a doctor for a problem and they ask, "well, you are 80, what do you expect at your age?" you might respond directly with, "I expect to be healthy and active, and that my physical complaints will be addressed, and not simply blamed on my age." In this case, the doctor's ageism minimizes the older person's health concerns and any related feelings about them.

Another example of being explicit is related to the attacks on Diversity, Equity and Inclusion, both in principle and in name. When someone says that they "oppose DEI," you might ask them to be more specific and to name the words individually. Do not allow the conversation to center around the acronym of DEI, but instead require the speaker to say which of the terms of diversity, equity, and inclusion are especially problematic for them. (Does this example make you feel defensive? Why or why not?)

One point to consider in conversation is to use "I" statements. Instead of saying things like, "You're being defensive," or "You always do this," focus on how you feel. For example, "I feel frustrated when I can't explain my point," or "I'm just trying to understand." Try asking open-ended questions to invite conversation. For example, "Can you help me understand why you're feeling this way?" or "What part of what I said didn't feel right to you?" For some people, open-ended questions represent opportunities for engagement, possibility, and flexibility. Sometimes this allows a person to avoid being painted into a corner.

Several psychological and educational theories support the idea that open-ended questions can promote deep thinking, creativity, and engagement. Open-ended questions stimulate critical thinking and self-reflection (Paul & Elder, 2007). Some scholars argue that open-ended questions encourage us to construct our own understanding (Vygotsky & Cole, 1978) and can foster adaptability and problem-solving when faced with complex questions (Spiro et al., 2012). Others suggest that open-ended questions enhance intrinsic motivation by fostering autonomy (Deci & Ryan, 2013).

However, it is important to remember that some people find open-ended questions threatening. Open-ended questions may require more mental effort compared to closed-ended ones, increasing cognitive strain (Sweller, 1988). Some individuals and cultures experience stress when faced with ambiguity (Hofstede, 1980). Open-ended questions might make people feel vulnerable, leading to defensive behavior (Gibb, 1961). Some people might experience open-ended questions as a threat to self-esteem or competence (Lazarus & Folkman, 1984). Others might feel that open-ended questions can feel invasive or challenging, making people defensive (Buller & Burgoon, 1996).

Perhaps consider how you feel about open-ended questions. Do you think your reactions to them change depending on the situation? On the topic? On the person with whom you are speaking? Do you think there is a relationship between these reactions and internalizing or externalizing reactions?

Sometimes people become defensive because they feel unheard or misunderstood. Acknowledge their feelings by saying something like, "I can see this is important to you," or "I understand why you might feel that way." People often get defensive when they feel blamed. Try to focus on the issue, not the person. For example, "The situation we're discussing is tough," instead of "You made this hard." If appropriate, offer a way forward or reassure them that you are on the same side. While you may have strong feelings of disagreement with the person you are speaking with, the only way to keep a healthy conversation going is to find points of connection. This does not mean that you have to agree with one another at all. Instead, the point is to find ways to keep the discussion going. This can help to shift the conversation from a defensive stance to a more cooperative one.

You may also need to set boundaries. If the discrimination continues or is subtle, it might be helpful to set clear boundaries. Let the person know what behavior or language is unacceptable and how it affects you. For instance, "I'd appreciate it if we could avoid comments like that" or "I'm not okay with being treated that way, and I need you to stop." In certain situations, humor can be a way to deflect discrimination and ease the tension. But this can be tricky and should only be done if you feel it won't downplay your feelings or make the situation worse. Encountering defensiveness in discrimination is emotionally draining. Be sure to take care of yourself afterward, whether by talking to someone you trust, engaging in a calming activity, or seeking professional support if needed.

Sometimes those boundaries mean disconnecting from the other person. This can be difficult and scary, especially depending on the nature of the relationship. There can be emotional, psychological, physical, and financial consequences to pulling away. However, when other boundaries have been unsuccessful, or the person is incapable or unwilling to respect your needs, your personal safety is always a priority. See a licensed mental health practitioner for more guidance.

FOCUS ON GROUPS

Another way to think about defensiveness is in the context of large groups. If you are a leader, you might need to think about the defensiveness of both individuals and groups in many different scenarios. You might be a teacher, office manager, project manager, coach, supervisor, chair of a committee, or in some other leadership position. Your team might split into cliques, your coworkers might be gridlocked on an ideological divide, or your organization might be operating based on decisions made over a rift that happened many years ago. Decision makers and others in positions of power might explore their investments and stakes in particular projects or positions. In doing so, they might also consider other positions present in the negotiations or team. If leaders examine their own defensiveness and can anticipate the defensive reactions of their team members, opponents, and allies, more effective leadership and action may result.

Sometimes this involves asking more questions and listening more carefully. You might hire consultants for your business or organization to assist in these conversations. Depending on your situation, you might consider a program evaluation, where a system process evaluates the effectiveness and efficiency of a program. You might learn that defensiveness and fissures in communication could play a role in a group dynamic.

In a famous social psychology experiment by Sherif (1988), researchers studied how intergroup conflict arises when groups compete for limited resources. In what is the classic "Robbers Cave Experiment" researchers placed boys into two random groups that were named the "Eagles" and "Rattlers." This study demonstrated that simply placing people in different groups can lead to hostility and prejudice between them. In this experiment, the boys were divided into the Eagles and the Rattlers, and their rivalry escalated when put into competitive situations. After the boys' hostility started to escalate, the researchers needed to repair the rupture to their relationships. In response, the boys were assigned tasks that required cooperation and interdependent tasks, and, as a consequence, the hostility diminished. Some researchers believe that while the original experiment had limitations, the lessons we learned from it continue to have applications for other contexts such as business workplaces and political conflicts (Onyango, 2023; Tyerman & Spencer, 1983). If you are a coach, teacher, or any leader of a group, you might consider delegating tasks and creating exercises that require cooperation. These activities could be specific to your work or learning environment, or you might get creative about ways that individuals and groups might "think outside the box" in order to foster interdependence and team-building. Create opportunities for employees from different parts of the team to work together on projects. This helps break down divisions and promotes understanding between individuals who may not usually interact. Consider rotating team roles or tasks to give employees a chance to collaborate with others outside their usual clique.

As a leader, model the behavior you want to see in your team. Encourage transparency and communication between team members (Bennis et al., 2008). Set up regular check-ins or meetings where everyone has a chance to speak and share updates. Ensure individuals feel comfortable discussing their thoughts and concerns without fear of punishment. Show inclusiveness in your own actions by interacting with all students or employees equally and avoiding favoritism. Make it clear that inclusivity is important. Set expectations for collaboration and respect. If cliques are forming in a way that is damaging to the climate, this should be addressed. If you notice a clique is starting to negatively affect the team or cause tension, address it head-on in a private, nonconfrontational way (Gaston, 2023; Gruenert & Whitaker, 2019). Speak to those involved individually or in small groups to understand the issue and come up with solutions. Organize team-building events or activities that encourage individuals to interact outside of their normal work, school, or team environment (Midura & Glover, 2005). This can help break down barriers and form new, positive connections.

Another strategy as a leader is to teach your group about defensiveness. For example, as a professor, I begin my courses with the content of this book in order to equip all of us, myself included, with more tools to navigate challenges that will arise in the class. Sometimes when a conversation gets sticky, or a student offers a prickly response, I suggest that we all refer to our defensiveness training to try to identify what is happening in the discussion. When watching a film or teaching a new, challenging concept, I ask students to have their notes on defensiveness handy so that we can integrate it into our learning. Questions to consider include: How do you notice defensiveness in yourself? Can you identify which type it might be? Can you recognize defensiveness in the room, in others? In the video, reading, or training materials? Can we apply the BEAR method here? What would that look like?

Taking the time to stop and unpack the psychological and emotional dynamics in the room can be challenging when time is limited. However, as a leader, it can model for others how to take responsibility for the process and not only the outcome. Integrating the vocabulary of defensiveness can help to name both obstacles and opportunities. Leaders can also emphasize the difference between feelings and behaviors. While anyone can have any feeling, these feelings do not justify harmful behaviors. We have choices in how to respond, which is different from reacting. We can take care of ourselves while also paying attention to how another person might feel.

Several psychological theories and research frameworks support the benefits of role-playing in addressing defensiveness. Role-playing allows participants to actively engage in learning, reducing defensiveness through real-world simulations (Kolb, 2014). As we have seen, people react defensively in groups when they feel evaluated or threatened. Role-playing can help individuals recognize defensive behaviors and develop more constructive responses (Gibb, 1961). Observing and practicing alternative behaviors in role-play can reduce defensiveness and promote empathy in group interactions (Bandura & Walters, 1977). Role-playing fosters self-awareness and emotional regulation, helping participants recognize and manage defensive reactions (Goleman, 2005).

One example of a famous role-play was the *Blue-Eyes/Brown-Eyes Experiment*, which was a social exercise conducted by Jane Elliott, a third-grade teacher in Iowa, in 1968. She designed it to teach her students about discrimination and prejudice the day after Martin Luther King Jr. was assassinated (Elliott, 2018). Elliott separated her all-white class into two groups based on eye color: blue-eyed children and brown-eyed children. On the first day, she told the class that blue-eyed children were superior—smarter, better, and more deserving of privileges. She gave them extra recess time, let them sit at the front of the class, and encouraged them to interact only with other blue-eyed children. She made the brown-eyed children wear collars to mark them as inferior. They were given fewer privileges and were often criticized or scolded more harshly. Within hours, the blue-eyed children became more confident, arrogant, and even mean toward their brown-eyed classmates. Meanwhile, the brown-eyed children became timid, insecure, and performed worse academically. The next day, Elliott switched the roles, telling the class that she had made a mistake and that brown-eyed children were actually superior. The same patterns emerged—this time with brown-eyed students acting dominant and blue-eyed students feeling discouraged. At the end, Elliott led a conversation about discrimination, helping students reflect on their experiences and how unfair it felt. See this link for a video: https://www.youtube.com/watch?v=1CtrpLh6TKk

Similar to the Robbers Cave, the experiment showed how quickly people can internalize superiority or inferiority based on arbitrary traits, highlighting the emotional and psychological effects of discrimination. Elliott demonstrated how easily prejudice can be taught and reinforced by authority figures. The students who participated in the experiment later reported that it had a lasting impact on their understanding of racism and bias (Peters, 1987). The exercise has since been replicated with adults, and Jane Elliott became a well-known advocate for antiracism education (Peters, 1987). However, the experiment has also been criticized for being emotionally intense, especially when conducted with young children (Bigler, 1999). Leaders might consider a version of this experiment that is tailored to the conditions and circumstances of their workplace, team, group, or classroom.

Leaders of groups can have more success overall by examining defensiveness. Understanding how people work while also engaging in critical self-reflection are qualities of successful leaders, contributing to attributes such as tolerance for ambiguity, openness, emotional stability, emotional intelligence, and conscientiousness (Zaccaro et al., 2013). If leaders examine their own defensiveness and can anticipate the defensive reactions of their team members, opponents, and allies, more effective leadership may result. For example, imagine an administrator wants to make a policy change. As we have seen, people often do not like change, no matter how big or small. The administrator might examine collective investments in the change, including their own. They might ask, how might others respond differently than I am to this change? What is at stake in keeping the old policy? Who might be defensive? How might that defensiveness arise? What is at stake if we change it? What might be some obstacles to the process? What reactions of others might be obstacles? With such information, the administrator might be able to present the policy change in a way that allows different voices to be heard while also addressing some anticipated fears and reactions.

By integrating vocabulary and skills around defensiveness into your leadership strategies, cultures of understanding and growth can be encouraged by normalizing defensive reactions (Brown, 2018). Part of this is knowing that change is a process, and that it will take time—time to learn about all sides and perspectives, time to navigate our own reactions, and time to consider what is realistic and what is not.

General Reflective Exercise

Name one way you will use this information in your personal life.

Name one way you will use this information in your work/school/professional life.

Exercise

Review the defense mechanisms. Consider all you have learned so far.

Imagine a friend is struggling with a difficult breakup. Based on what you now know about defense mechanisms, how might they respond using different mechanisms?

- How could understanding these mechanisms help you better support them?
- Identify one or two defense mechanisms you use frequently.
- Consider a healthier coping strategy you could try instead.
- Write a short reflection (three to five sentences) on how increasing awareness of your defense mechanisms might improve your emotional well-being and relationships.

SUMMARY

In this chapter, we explored practical strategies for implementation beyond naming including reframing devices such as pausing, breathing, asking questions, education, data collection, cultivating curiosity, bidirectional identification of defensiveness (in both parties, not just one), attitude adjustment, and suggestions for language and negotiation. We examined how to focus on defensiveness in ourselves, others, and groups. Of course, this discussion is not exhaustive. Ideally, this is a lifelong process of change and growth. Keep practicing all your skills, knowing that you cannot be perfect. You will make mistakes, and you can make a commitment to keep learning. Chapter 5 will discuss myths, future directions, and final thoughts.

General Exercises on Defense Mechanisms

Consider exercises and activities from:

- Defense Mechanisms Worksheets: 10 Tools for Practitioner (https://positivepsychology.com/defense-mechanism-worksheets/#worksheet)
- For thinking about defensiveness in a digital world as a result of the pandemic: Digital Dilemmas-Harvard University (handout)

(https://pz.harvard.edu/sites/default/files/Digital%20Dilemma%20-%20Social%20Media%20and%20COVID-19.pdf)

- For a video on different kinds of violence (with implications for defensiveness) Direct structural, cultural violence (2:10) (https://www.youtube.com/watch?v=LW_rTeawAi0)

Chapter 5
Conclusion

Dr. Felix opens class with a prompt:
    "What's something you believed deeply about yourself that you now question?"
    The room is quiet, pencils scratching. Some students look around, gauging whether it's safe to be honest.
    Lark shares first: "That I had to 'make sense' to be real."
    Leah follows: "That my good intentions were enough."
    Carter: "That being strong means being silent."
    Tasha: "That being successful meant shrinking."
    Darius waits, then quietly says: "That being angry makes me dangerous."
    A hush falls over the room. For a moment, it's not a classroom—it's a circle. A space of breath and truth.
    Dr. Felix sets down her marker.
    "You're doing the work," she says. "You're showing up. That's more than most."

As I mentioned at the beginning of this guidebook, I first learned about defense mechanisms in an introductory psychology class. I have continued to learn about them every day since. Defense mechanisms, while often operating beneath the surface of awareness, shape the way we cope, connect, and construct meaning in our lives. As we have explored throughout this guidebook, these unconscious psychological strategies can serve both healthy and less

Transforming Defensiveness: A Guidebook for Rewriting Our Stories & Reclaiming Connection, First Edition. Andrea L. Dottolo.
© 2026 John Wiley & Sons, Inc. All rights reserved, including rights for text and data mining and training of artificial intelligence technologies or similar technologies.
Published 2026 by John Wiley & Sons, Inc.

healthy roles—shielding us from emotional pain, preserving self-image, and influencing behavior in subtle yet profound ways. In this chapter, we will review some myths about defensiveness, final thoughts, and future directions.

MYTHS ABOUT DEFENSIVENESS

Just the idea of talking about defensiveness can sometimes make people feel defensive. This is just one of many reasons why there are many myths and misconceptions about defensiveness. With ignorance and anxiety, misinformation can grow (Salecl, 2022). As we review what we have learned, let's unpack some of these myths—to dispel misconceptions, foster clarity, and encourage curiosity. As you review each one, consider if you or anyone you know might endorse these myths.

Myth #1: Defensiveness Is Always a Choice

One of the more important elements of understanding defense mechanisms is that they operate at an *unconscious* level, or outside of our awareness. They function to *protect* us from distressing thoughts or emotions. There are several reasons why this myth is so popular. When we think about the idea of *protecting ourselves,* it is often in a way that feels conscious, or something that we choose to do. For example, if I see a driver on the highway speeding and weaving in and out of traffic, I might notice them and willfully slow down, consciously taking my foot off the accelerator as a way to avoid a potentially dangerous and threatening situation. I am actively trying to protect myself (and possibly other drivers) from a bad accident. My behavior is likely perceived by myself and others as intentional. This is a choice.

Another reason that this myth that defensiveness is a choice is popular is that in Western cultures, we center individuals and individualistic values. In particular, psychology as a discipline often blames the stresses, challenges, and problems that people face on the individual. Kitzinger (1987) labeled this tendency of psychologists to focus on "individuocentricity," where internal processes such as thoughts and feelings are emphasized over the institutional or social structures in which a person lives. When someone is feeling depressed, we live in a culture that tends to have a knee-jerk reaction to want to prescribe drugs. This doesn't mean that antidepressants or other pharmaceuticals aren't helpful to lots of people. However, by examining the social situations and living conditions of a person first, we might discover that they have good reason to be depressed, and that they are not necessarily suffering from a "chemical imbalance." They might be carrying lots of stress at work, struggling to pay their bills, or grieving the death of a loved one. Because we tend to highlight the role of the individual while minimizing larger social factors, we imagine or assume that everyone has similar choices.

Americans in particular hold the value of the "American Dream," or the idea that if you work hard, you will be rewarded. This belief carries with it the accompanying conviction that if someone is struggling or suffering, they must deserve it. Americans often endorse statements that claim that complicated conditions like poverty are a choice (Cozzarelli et al., 2001). In other words, we tend to center our explanations for why individuals live the way they do based on their own "free will."

It makes sense then, that when we observe someone's behavior, we believe that they are in charge, that they made a choice. However, our brains are sophisticated machines, often working outside of our awareness, to defend us from danger. Sometimes we aren't even aware that we perceive a danger, but our brains detected the threat and "took over" to make sure that we are safe. For example, a person might refuse to believe that a loved one has died and continue to set a place for them at the dinner table. This is an illustration of *denial*, where a person refuses to admit or accept a reality because it is too threatening or painful. People often confuse denial with simply being stubborn or willfully ignorant. However, denial is usually an unconscious refusal to face something overwhelming, not a conscious choice to ignore reality.

Now here's where there's some wiggle room in the myth. One of the "tricks" to the myth is that defensiveness is *always* a choice (which it is not). It is likely that the first time the person set the table for their loved one, it was an automatic behavior, almost like a reflex. But here's the key: once they become *aware* (or conscious) of their unconscious response, then they can change it. They can make a choice to behave differently in the future, but only once they understand what they did and why they did it.

Furthermore, some types of defense mechanisms are more conscious than others. One form, called *unintentionality,* is when someone claims that they "don't mean" to cause harm, but then they go ahead and say something hurtful. For example, if someone says, "I don't mean to be rude, but …" or "no offense, but …"—these are often phrases that precede a rude or offensive statement. In other words, the speaker is *aware* that what they are saying might be inappropriate or harmful because they announce it beforehand.

The myth that defensiveness is always a choice illustrates the complexity of both *how* our minds work, alongside our *beliefs* about how the mind works. While most defense mechanisms are unconscious, once we are aware of them, we can make change. Many people don't want to believe that they are not in complete control of their behaviors and that they are always exercising their right to choose. Even considering these ideas can sometimes trigger defensiveness.

As you continue to explore defensiveness, perhaps pay attention to how your body responds. Do you notice your chest tighten sometimes? Or an "icky" feeling in your stomach? Do you ever feel like you are getting warm? Does your breath quicken? Does it get shallow? Can you feel your jaw clench? Do your shoulders start to creep up toward your ears? These are all common bodily responses to defensiveness. Focusing on the body as a kind of alarm or warning sign can encourage us to consider different ways of responding.

Case Study 5.1 "Feedback for Maya"

BACKGROUND

Maya, a 34-year-old elementary school teacher, is known among her colleagues as passionate and dedicated, but also occasionally "hard to talk to" during staff meetings. She was recently given performance feedback by her principal, who noted that Maya seemed to "get defensive whenever her methods are questioned."

Maya's initial reaction to this feedback was denial and frustration. "I'm not defensive," she told a coworker. "They just don't understand how hard I work." This reaction further reinforced the perception among her peers that she couldn't take criticism.

THE TRIGGER

During a professional development session, the group was discussing classroom management strategies. When another teacher casually commented that Maya's classroom seemed "chaotic at times," Maya immediately responded with a sharp tone:

"Well, maybe if you had 28 kids with IEPs, you'd understand."

She later left the meeting abruptly, visibly upset.

THE DEEPER STORY

In therapy, Maya began unpacking why she reacts so strongly in these moments. Through trauma-informed counseling, she came to understand that her defensiveness wasn't a conscious choice—it was rooted in her past.

As a child, Maya was frequently criticized and belittled by a parent with high expectations. Any mistake was treated as a failure, and emotional safety was often missing. Over time, she developed an automatic survival response: any critique, even mild or well intentioned, triggered feelings of shame, fear, and a fight-or-flight response. Her brain interpreted feedback as a threat—not because she wanted to feel defensive, but because her nervous system was wired to protect her.

INSIGHTS GAINED

Maya's therapy helped her develop more awareness of these patterns. She began learning to pause, breathe, and recognize when her reaction was protective rather than intentional. Her principal, upon learning more about trauma-informed communication, also adjusted their approach—offering feedback in private, using validating language, and giving Maya space to reflect before responding.

CONCLUSION

Maya's case illustrates that defensiveness is not always a conscious decision. Notice how this is connected to Myth #1: Defensiveness is always a choice. It is important to remember that defense can be a deeply conditioned, physiological response to past emotional wounding. With support and understanding, both Maya and her workplace were able to shift the dynamic from judgment to growth.

Myth #2: Defense Mechanisms Are Always Bad or a Sign of Mental Illness

Many people think that defense mechanisms are always unhealthy or signs of emotional problems, but that's not true. As you have learned, defense mechanisms are normal and even helpful ways our brains protect us from stress, fear, or sadness. We all use them, even if we don't realize it. According to Vaillant (1992), some defense mechanisms can even help people become more emotionally strong. For example, when people use humor or plan ahead to deal with challenges, they are using positive, mature defenses.

Defense mechanisms help us keep our emotions balanced, especially when things feel overwhelming. Someone might avoid thinking about a sad event just so they can get through the day. That's not necessarily a bad thing—it may help them function until they are ready to deal with their feelings. Cramer (2006) explains that defense mechanisms only become a problem when they are used too often, in the wrong situations, or if they stop us from growing emotionally.

Remember displacement? This is when someone takes out their feelings on someone or something safer, instead of facing the real cause of stress. Jordan has a tough day at work, feels overwhelmed, and then yells at their roommate about something small. They're not really angry about the mess—it's more about everything they bottled up during the day. Displacement helped Jordan release tension, but it hurt their roommate and didn't solve the real problem.

This is why it's important to understand that defense mechanisms are often unconscious—we don't always know we're using them. Once we become aware of what we're doing and how it affects others, we can make better choices. According to Baumeister et al. (1994), recognizing our defenses can help us grow, take responsibility, and respond in healthier ways. So, instead of calling defense mechanisms "bad," we should learn how to use them wisely.

Exercise

Scenario: The Team Meeting

You're in a team meeting at work. You've spent the past week preparing a detailed presentation with new ideas for improving a workflow. When it's your turn to present, one of your colleagues interrupts halfway through and says:

> "Honestly, I don't think this is practical at all. We've tried similar things before and they never work."

You immediately feel your body tense up. Your heart beats faster. You feel the urge to cross your arms, correct them sharply, or even withdraw from the conversation.

Step 1: Identify the Response

How do you imagine you'd feel in that moment?
(Think about emotions, physical sensations, or automatic thoughts.)

What would your first instinct be?
(Interrupt them back? Shut down? Defend your work? Something else?)

Step 2: Explore the Defensiveness
What might your defensiveness be trying to protect in this situation?
- Your credibility?
- Your sense of competence?
- Your effort and time?
- A core value (e.g., being taken seriously, being collaborative)?

Is there something valuable or true within your defensive reaction? What might it be pointing to?

Step 3: Reframe the Reaction
Now imagine you take a breath and pause before responding.

If you treated your defensiveness as a helpful signal instead of a problem, how might you respond differently?

What could a balanced response look like—one that respects your boundaries without escalating tension?

Step 4: Personal Reflection
Have you ever had a real-life situation like this, where you felt defensive but later realized it was revealing something important to you?

Looking back, how did that defensiveness help you (or how *could* it have helped you) set boundaries, communicate values, or recognize something meaningful?

Optional Activity
Draw or write a comic strip showing someone using a defense mechanism, realizing it, and trying a new way to respond. This helps show emotional growth.

Myth #3: Defensiveness Is the Same as Aggression

Many people think that when someone is defensive, they're automatically being rude or aggressive. But that's not always true. Defensiveness can show up in many different ways—some loud and some quiet. While some people may raise their voice, others might stay silent, avoid the topic, or act like nothing is wrong. This does not mean they are not feeling upset; it just means they're showing it in a different way. According to Bond (2004), not all defenses look like anger. Some are passive, like denial (refusing to believe something is true) or intellectualization (overthinking without feeling emotions).

It's important to understand that defensiveness is about protecting ourselves from emotional pain, not always about attacking others. When someone feels hurt, judged, or afraid, their brain might try to "shield" them by reacting defensively. As Baumeister et al. (1994) explained, people sometimes act defensively to protect their sense of identity or self-worth. This is often unconscious, under the surface of their awareness—they're just trying to feel safe in the moment.

Let's look at a classroom example. Imagine a student gets feedback on a project and hears, "You did a good job, but your sources could be stronger." Instead of saying, "Thanks, I'll work on that," the student says, "Well, I didn't have time because I had practice, and no one explained how to do it right." At this point, the professor reminded the student that instructions were covered in class on how to do the assignment, specifically on how to cite sources. The student's reaction isn't only aggression—it's also defensiveness. The student might feel embarrassed or afraid of looking "not smart," so they defend themselves by making excuses. They're not trying to be mean—they're trying to protect how they see themselves. However, the student may benefit from reflecting on how their reaction might have been received by the professor, and how to better choose behaviors that could serve their best interests in the future.

Aggression can sometimes come after defensiveness, especially when people feel backed into a corner or misunderstood. But defensiveness itself is much broader than just anger. It can include fear, sadness, guilt, or shame. As Cramer (2006) points out, defense mechanisms are part of how humans deal with emotional stress. Understanding the difference between aggression and defensiveness helps us respond with compassion instead of judgment.

Case Study 5.2 "Ava's Art Grade"
SCENARIO

Ava is a student who puts a lot of effort into her schoolwork. One day, she turns in an art project and gets a B+. Her teacher writes, "Great creativity! Try working on shading techniques next time." Ava immediately frowns

> and says, "I don't see what's wrong with it. I worked really hard, and not everyone's an art expert."
>
> **WHAT'S HAPPENING?**
> Ava is responding defensively. Her response isn't meant to be an attack on the teacher—it's her way of handling the disappointment. She's protecting her self-image as a hardworking student and doesn't want to feel like she failed.

Reflective Exercise: "What's Under the Surface?"

Now, answer the following questions:

1. How is Ava feeling on the inside?
2. What do you think Ava is trying to protect?
3. Have you ever gotten feedback and felt upset—even if it was helpful?
4. Did you show your feelings or hide them?
5. What is a more helpful way Ava could respond next time?
6. What would you say to Ava to help her feel supported?

Extension Activity

Write a short dialogue between Ava and her teacher, showing how they can have a kind, honest conversation where Ava expresses her feelings and the teacher offers support.

Myth #4: Only "Weak" People Are Defensive

Another misconception is that being defensive means someone is weak, fragile, or insecure. But this idea is not true. Being defensive does not mean a person lacks strength; it means they are trying to cope with something hard. Even people who are very confident may feel the need to protect themselves emotionally.

For example, an established teacher who is used to being evaluated regularly might still feel nervous when they get tough criticism. Instead of showing fear, they might make jokes or change the subject to avoid uncomfortable feelings. This is a kind of defense that helps them manage their emotions while still staying in control. Instead of thinking someone is "weak" because they get defensive, we can realize they might be feeling vulnerable or stressed. This understanding can create more empathy between people and allow room for kindness and support. As Cramer (2006) points out, recognizing how defense mechanisms work helps us grow emotionally and relate better to others.

Finally, when we stop labeling defensiveness as a flaw, we open the door to learning how to use defenses in healthier ways. It's okay to protect ourselves, but it's also important to become aware of when defenses become too strong or cause problems. This awareness can help us respond better to challenges and build stronger relationships (Vaillant, 1992).

Case Study 5.3 Lee's Crossed Arms

SCENARIO

Lee is a successful business manager who has to give a big presentation. When a colleague suggests a change to his plan, Lee immediately scowls, crosses his arms, and says, "I think my plan is perfect as it is." Later, he jokes about how nobody can criticize him without facing his "fierce reactions." Lee feels tense but hides his anxiety behind jokes and quick refusals.

WHAT'S HAPPENING?

Lee is being defensive, but that doesn't mean he's weak. He's trying to protect himself from feeling judged or uncertain. His jokes and quick replies are ways to manage stress and maintain confidence, even if he doesn't fully feel it inside.

1. What might Lee be feeling? (scared, embarrassed, angry, etc.?)
2. How did he react?
3. Do you think his reaction helped protect him?
4. What would have happened if he didn't protect himself this way?

Myth #5: Getting Rid of All Defenses Should Be the Goal of Therapy

This myth is the belief that when someone goes to therapy, the goal is to completely get rid of all their defense mechanisms. According to research in psychodynamic therapy, the real goal of therapy is not to eliminate these defenses, but to help people become aware of them and use them in healthier ways (Cramer, 2006). This means that instead of trying to erase defenses completely, therapy encourages people to change how they react to difficult emotions so they can handle them better.

Someone who always denies feeling sad may, over time, learn to accept and express those feelings openly. This shift is not about getting rid of defense mechanisms but about growing emotionally and learning to manage feelings in a mature way (Perry & Bond, 2012). Therapy helps people recognize these behaviors so they can choose healthier ways to cope, rather than being controlled by unconscious defenses. The work of therapy, and even society as a whole, should be about understanding and accepting these defenses instead of shaming them. By debunking myths about defensiveness and understanding its purpose, we can cultivate a better understanding of why therapy may be useful for many people, even those who may not have considered it before.

Case Study 5.4 "Emily is 'fine'"

Emily has always avoided talking about her feelings, especially when she feels sad or stressed. When her friends ask how she is, she often says, "I'm fine," even if she's upset. This is denial, which helps Emily avoid feeling overwhelmed by difficult emotions. When she starts therapy, Emily learns that denial is protecting her from pain, but it's also keeping her from connecting with her true feelings and with others.

Over time, with the help of her therapist, Emily begins to notice when she is denying her emotions. She practices naming her feelings and sharing them with trusted friends and family. This change does not mean Emily's defenses disappear; instead, she learns to use her defenses in a healthier way by being honest about her feelings when she feels safe. Emily's story shows how therapy can help people grow emotionally by changing how they use their defense mechanisms, not by getting rid of them completely.

Scenario Exercise: *Seeing the Good in Defensiveness*

Pat is in a therapy session. She's been meeting with her therapist for a few weeks to explore some relationship challenges and patterns of self-doubt. Today, the therapist brings up something Pat mentioned during last session—how she often feels "rejected" or "not listened to" by her partner.

As they gently ask a follow-up question to go deeper, Pats feels herself getting irritated and pulling back.

Scene: In the Therapist's Office

THERAPIST: "Last time, you said it really hurt when your partner dismissed your idea during that conversation. Can we explore what that brought up for you emotionally?"

PAT: (Quickly) "I mean, it's not that deep. I'm probably just overreacting anyway. It's not like I haven't dealt with worse."

THERAPIST: (pauses gently, then says) "I noticed you shifted just now—you brushed it off pretty quickly. That might be a kind of defensiveness coming up. That's not a bad thing—it often shows up to protect something important. Let's slow down a bit. Can we look at what that part of you might be trying to guard?"

Reflective Questions

What do you notice about Pat's reaction in this moment?

- What feelings came up for her when the therapist asked to go deeper?
- Do you think Pat felt vulnerable, exposed, or uncomfortable?

Why might defensiveness have shown up here?

- Was it protecting Pat from feeling judged? From feeling weak or ashamed? From opening up too quickly?

What could Pat's defensiveness be communicating for her that she hasn't yet put into words?

Reframing Defensiveness as Useful

Imagine the therapist continues:

"It sounds like that defensive part of you might be trying to keep you safe from emotional pain—or from repeating an old wound. What if we got curious about what it's protecting, rather than pushing it away?"

How could Pat's defensiveness signal an emotional boundary that she wasn't ready to cross? Could it help her to identify a tender spot that needs compassion? Could it help her to pace her emotional work safely?

What would it look like for Pat to *listen to her* defensiveness, rather than silence it?

Defensiveness isn't a wall—it's a doorway. When we explore it with care, it can lead us to the parts of ourselves that need understanding, safety, and healing. Understanding the myths surrounding defensiveness—such as the belief that it's inherently bad, that only "weak" people are defensive, or that it always shows up as aggression—helps us develop a more compassionate and nuanced perspective. These misconceptions often cause people to hide or feel ashamed of their defensive reactions, when in reality, defenses are normal and even necessary parts of human psychology. Recognizing their function and variability allows us to notice not just when they happen, but *why* they happen, and how they may be shaped by our environment. As our environments change, so too do the forms and triggers of defensiveness.

DEFENSIVENESS IN A DIGITAL AGE

One of the most powerful changes in our environment is the rise of digital technology and social media. Platforms like TikTok, Instagram, X (formerly Twitter), and Facebook have reshaped how we communicate, form identities, and engage with conflict. While digital tools allow for rapid connection and information-sharing, they also amplify emotional reactions and misunderstandings. In this increasingly digital world, defensiveness is not only more visible—it is often magnified by online norms, algorithms, and anonymity. In the next section, we will explore how defensiveness manifests in digital spaces, why it becomes so intense, and what strategies we can use to better navigate online dialogue and disagreement.

How Social Media Changes the Way We React to Ideas

The internet—and especially social media—has changed how people talk about important topics like politics, justice, or even personal opinions. Apps (or digital applications like the ones mentioned earlier, and also including Snapchat and YouTube) make it very easy for people to quickly share what they think or feel. This can be a good thing because it gives more people a voice. But it also creates a space where emotions can take over logic. For example, someone might see a post that challenges their beliefs and immediately respond with anger or sarcasm, instead of thinking it through calmly.

This rapid and emotional reaction happens often because social media rewards attention-getting behavior with likes, comments, or shares.

One reason strong emotions are so common online is because people often end up in **echo chambers**. This means they mostly hear and see opinions that match what they already believe. Social media algorithms are designed to show you posts with which you are likely to agree or interact. If you often watch videos about how one political party is right, the app will likely show you more videos that support that party and less information that challenges it. A study by Bakshy et al. (2015) found that Facebook users mostly saw political content that matched their beliefs, making them less likely to learn other perspectives. This makes it harder to understand or empathize with people who think differently.

Another problem is the **backfire effect**. This happens when people hear facts that go against what they believe, and instead of changing their minds, they actually hold onto their old beliefs even more strongly. If someone believes a false rumor about vaccines and is shown clear evidence that it is not true, they might feel attacked and become more convinced their belief is correct. Nyhan and Reifler (2010) studied this effect and found it often happened during political debates. Instead of helping people learn, new information can make them feel unsafe or challenged, leading them to defend their opinions even more strongly.

Another reason people react so strongly online is the **online disinhibition effect**. This means people feel more free to make comments online—especially ones that are mean or rude—that they would not say face-to-face. Because they can hide behind a screen or use a fake name, they feel less pressure to be polite or kind. According to Suler (2004), this often leads to impulsive comments, harsh criticism, or angry arguments. For instance, someone might call another person stupid in a comment thread but would never say that in person. This behavior adds to the tension and defensiveness we often see online.

All of these effects—echo chambers, the backfire effect, and online disinhibition—create a digital world where people are more likely to react than to reflect. That means people often respond with emotion rather than reason, and they defend their beliefs instead of listening to others. This creates a cycle of defensiveness, where individuals are not learning from each other—they are just trying to "win" arguments or prove their side is "right." Breaking this cycle requires patience, empathy, and learning to pause before reacting.

Case Study 5.5 "Jennifer and TikTok"

BACKGROUND
Jennifer is a 14-year-old who enjoys scrolling through TikTok in the evenings. One day, she sees a video claiming that a certain cultural group is responsible for many recent problems in society. The video uses emotional music and scary headlines to make its point. Jennifer watches a few more videos from the same creator and begins to believe the message.

CONFLICT
Later, her classmate Arjun posts a different video showing facts from trusted news sources that disagree with what Jennifer has seen. Jennifer immediately feels angry. Instead of considering Arjun's video, she comments: "You're just blind to what's really going on!" She even shares another video supporting her view, adding a defensive caption. Her reaction surprises Arjun, who had hoped to have a respectful conversation.

ANALYSIS
Jennifer's behavior is a mix of all three digital effects. She was in an **echo chamber**, only seeing one side of the issue. When faced with facts that challenged her views, she experienced the **backfire effect**, doubling down instead of reflecting. Because she was online, the **disinhibition effect** made it easier for her to react harshly and emotionally. Jennifer did not pause to ask herself whether her reaction was helping or hurting the conversation.

Reflective Exercise: "Pause, Reflect, Respond"

Scenario to Imagine
You see a post online that strongly disagrees with something you believe. Your first reaction is to type an angry comment. But instead of sending it, you decide to pause.

Step-by-Step Activity
1. **Pause**—Take 30 seconds before you respond.

2. **Reflect**—Ask yourself:
    - Is this post coming from someone in an echo chamber, or am I?
    - Am I feeling defensive because my belief is being challenged?
    - Would I say this comment to someone's face?
    - What emotion am I feeling right now—anger, fear, confusion?
3. **Respond**—Try writing a comment that asks a question or shares your view respectfully. For example: "I see we have different opinions. Can you tell me more about where you heard this?"

Journal Prompt
- Write about a time you felt defensive online.
- What were you defending? Did the other person's post make you feel attacked?
- Looking back, how could you have responded differently?

As digital platforms continue to shape how we express ourselves and relate to others, they also play a powerful role in influencing our political attitudes and behaviors. The same online dynamics that heighten emotional reactivity—such as echo chambers, anonymity, and algorithmic reinforcement—have become deeply entangled with political discourse. In today's polarized landscape, political identity is often tied to personal identity, making disagreements feel not just ideological but deeply personal. As we shift from exploring defensiveness in a digital age to its role in contemporary politics, we will examine how psychological defenses emerge in response to perceived threats to group belonging, moral identity, and institutional trust—creating a political climate that is increasingly reactive, fragmented, and resistant to dialogue.

DEFENSIVENESS IN TODAY'S POLITICAL CLIMATE

Today's political discussions can feel intense and personal. That's because many people connect their political beliefs with who they are as individuals. When someone questions or challenges those beliefs, it may feel like they are attacking you as a person. This can make it very hard to have calm, respectful conversations, especially online. What looks like strong conviction is often a form of defensiveness—a way to protect one's identity from emotional discomfort or perceived threats (Westen, 2007).

One example of this is called the **hostile media effect**. This happens when people see news stories that are meant to be fair or neutral but feel as though the stories are biased against their side. Vallone et al. (1985) conducted a study that demonstrated how individuals' preexisting beliefs can strongly influence their perception of media bias. In their research, both pro-Israel and pro-Arab participants were shown the same news footage covering the conflict in the Middle East. Remarkably, members of each group perceived the coverage as being biased against their own side, despite viewing identical content. This phenomenon, known as the hostile media effect, illustrates a broader psychological tendency: people often interpret neutral or balanced reporting as biased if it does not align with their personal views. In other words, individuals may distrust or criticize the media simply because it fails to fully support their preferred perspective, not necessarily because the reporting is actually unfair. This has important implications for understanding political polarization and the challenges of trust in journalism in increasingly divided societies.

Political groups also give people a sense of belonging, purpose, and moral goodness. When these groups are criticized—for example, being called sexist, racist, or unfair—people may feel personally attacked. This triggers what psychologists call **ingroup defensiveness**. We discussed this earlier in our conversation of in-group bias. According to Branscombe et al. (1999), when a group's image is threatened, its members often dismiss the criticism and defend their group more strongly. If a political group is accused of supporting unfair laws, its followers may double down and blame the other side instead of reflecting on the issue.

Another problem in today's digital world is the fear of speaking up. Some people are scared to share their opinions online because they worry about being judged, losing friends, or even getting in trouble. This leads to something called **self-censorship**. A study by Hayes et al. (2005) found that people are less likely to speak their minds when they believe most others disagree with them. For instance, a student might not say what they really think about a protest or political event in a classroom discussion or on social media, fearing backlash. This creates the illusion that everyone agrees, even when they do not.

In all of these examples, defensiveness shapes how we talk about politics. Whether it's distrusting the news, protecting a group's image, or staying silent out of fear, these reactions often come from an emotional place. While it is understandable to feel strongly about your beliefs, it is also important to recognize when defensiveness is making it harder to listen, learn, or grow. Being aware of these patterns can help us become more respectful and open minded, especially in political conversations that matter deeply to us and to society as a whole.

Case Study 5.6 A Conversation at the Community Center

SCENARIO

Nancy, a retired teacher in her late 60s, attends a discussion group at her local community center. The group is reviewing a newspaper article that highlights problems within a political party Nancy strongly supports. Although the article presents facts from multiple perspectives, Nancy immediately becomes upset and says, "This paper has always had it out for us—this is completely one-sided reporting."

Another participant, Thomas, a retired postal worker, gently adds, "I've supported that party for years too, but I think it's fair to admit they've made some mistakes. We should be willing to talk about them."

Nancy responds sharply, "It's people like you turning on your own side that let the other party win!"

ANALYSIS

Nancy's reaction shows signs of the **hostile media effect**—believing the news is biased just because it doesn't reflect her views. Her quick defense of the political group, and harsh response to Thomas, reflect **ingroup defensiveness**. She perceives Thomas's thoughtful critique as a betrayal, rather than a constructive conversation. Her defensiveness may also make others in the group afraid to share differing opinions, leading to **self-censorship** and limiting honest dialogue.

Reflective Exercise: Understanding Defensiveness in Political Discussions

Objective

To explore how emotional reactions in political discussions may be driven by defensiveness and how awareness can lead to more respectful and open conversations.

Step 1: Reflect on the Case Study
Read or recall the scenario with Nancy and Thomas.

Questions for Reflection
1. Why do you think Nancy felt the article was biased?
2. What emotions might Nancy be feeling underneath her reaction (e.g., fear, loyalty, frustration)?
3. Was Thomas trying to attack Nancy or her political views?
4. How might Nancy's response affect the tone of the group discussion?
5. Have you ever been in a situation where someone challenged your views? How did it feel?

Step 2: Personal Connection
Journal Prompt
Think about a time when you felt defensive during a conversation—maybe about politics, family, or another important topic.

- What triggered your reaction?
- What were you protecting?
- How did the other person respond?
- Looking back, is there anything you might do differently?

Step 3: Practicing a New Response
Scenario Activity
Imagine you are Nancy, but this time, take a deep breath after hearing Thomas's comment. You decide to respond differently.

Write a few sentences of a calm, curious reply you could give.
For example:

"That's a fair point, Thomas. I guess I just feel upset when I hear criticism because I've supported this group for so long. But maybe it's worth looking at what can be improved."

Then, write a sentence Thomas could say in response that keeps the conversation respectful and open.

DEFENSIVENESS AND ARTIFICIAL INTELLIGENCE: A SPECIAL CASE
Public Anxiety and Institutional Trust

As artificial intelligence (AI) becomes a bigger part of life—helping doctors diagnose illnesses or helping stores manage deliveries—many people feel nervous or unsure. While AI can be helpful, not everyone trusts it. For example, the Brookings Institution (2022) and Pew Research Center (2023) found that people often feel torn. Some are hopeful about the benefits, but many worry about job loss, privacy, and being watched by machines. People who don't trust the government or big companies, or who feel they cannot control technology, are more likely to react defensively (Nye et al., 1997). This means they may want to stop AI from growing, even if they don't fully understand how it works.

A community that recently lost jobs to automation might protest the use of AI at their local hospital, believing it will replace nurses—even if that's not true. This kind of fear is called **existential defensiveness**. It's not just about fearing a robot or machine—it's about feeling that your way of life is being threatened. When people feel powerless, they may ask for bans or strict rules, even if they don't know all the facts. Think of how some people wanted to ban all self-driving cars after hearing about a single accident. Even though studies show that self-driving cars could be safer in the long run, the fear was stronger than the facts (Floridi et al., 2018). Existential defensiveness can help protect people emotionally, but it can also block helpful progress.

NARRATIVE DEFENSE AND THE POWER OF STORYTELLING

Our beliefs about AI don't just come from facts—they also come from stories we've seen in movies or on TV. Shows like *Black Mirror* or movies like *The Terminator* have painted AI as scary and dangerous, where robots and advanced technologies are threatening, cause harm, and foster a fear of loss of control. These stories stick in our minds, even if they are not realistic. When real AI systems, like a chatbot or smart assistant, act in ways that do not match those stories, people often feel uncomfortable or confused. This is called

narrative defensiveness (McAdams & Janis, 2004). For example, when a helpful AI tool recommends music or news articles, someone might still worry it is spying on them—because they have seen too many scary tech stories. These fears make it hard to accept AI as a tool.

It seems important to share some of my own defensive responses to AI, specifically as it relates to my teaching and in writing this book. A few years ago, I began to notice a huge increase in what seemed to me to be plagiarism in student assignments. Of course, a few students have always copied ideas from elsewhere, whether it was textbooks or the internet, and these rare instances are usually relatively easy to detect. However, this one semester about 25% of all of my students were submitting assignments that were obviously not written by them, using language and phrasing that they could not possibly know or understand. When confronted, most admitted it, especially when I asked them to explain particular phrasing (like the "bifurcation of gender") that they had written into their own words, and they could not do it. Some students did not admit their wrongdoing, but doubled down their insistence that it was their own writing, despite their inability to explain what they claimed were their own words. At first, I gave every student an opportunity to resubmit their papers. Many did, and still a few others simply handed in AI-written papers again.

As an instructor who is truly committed to my students and their learning, I was devastated. I asked them individually and collectively what was happening. I was scared, desperate, sad, and outraged. I told them that I could understand if I were teaching courses that tested fact-based knowledge, or courses that were simply requirements outside of their major, in which they had no interest. But I teach largely upper-level undergraduate courses in psychology, where students enroll because they are interested in a career in the field, often as future therapists. The curriculum is geared toward teaching them real-world skills to use in their chosen professions and their own lives (such as how to understand defensiveness!). Some students apologized. Some sheepishly resubmitted their papers. Others gave up and failed the course.

I was in the middle of my own existential and narrative defensiveness. I wondered if I should quit my job, if my profession is obsolete, or if I could survive in a new version of this digital age. (For the record, I still ponder these points regularly.) I devoted that summer to redesigning my courses, assignments, and assessments. I researched how to teach with AI; joined working groups, trainings, and discussions; and consulted with other faculty and colleagues. I now understand that AI is simply a new tool, and now I integrate it into my teaching in classroom exercises and writing assignments. I also evaluate learning more heavily on old-fashioned, paper-and-pencil writing in class, presentations, and creative, hands-on projects. But this process took a while. And I'm still scared and learning, especially as the technology changes, grows, shifts, and transforms right before our eyes.

Shortly thereafter, I began writing this book. This book is the culmination of over two decades of teaching and learning, so I wrote it in my own voice, from my own lens. And then I learned that I could also use AI as a tool. At first I was terrified, not only because of my own experience with my students, but convinced I would certainly be arrested by the "plagiarism police." I avoided even opening any AI platforms. And then I met with other authors and editors, and, again, learned that as long as I was using it as a tool, it could be "acceptable." For example, I would write a passage and ask AI to clean up the language, or offer another example of a concept. I asked AI to provide descriptive detail to case studies, or to reword passages into less formal, more accessible language. These are also the kinds of tasks I would ask friends and colleagues to do for me in the past, as they read my drafts and offered feedback. Now, I could get instant responses and not have to bother anyone else.

Sometimes AI was awful. It produced simply inaccurate content. Or worse (as I discuss in my classes), racist, sexist, and homophobic statements. Sometimes AI invented scholarly resources that simply don't exist. It often wrote in a voice that didn't sound like me, so there was lots of editing, deleting, and revising. But overall, AI changed the way I think about teaching and writing. And, as I continue this learning process, I have also come to understand that humans are still necessary in doing the thinking in using this powerful tool. I learned about prompt engineering, which is the practice of crafting and refining the input (called a *prompt*) given to an AI model—like ChatGPT—to guide it toward producing a desired response. Because AI models respond based on the patterns they learned during training, the way you phrase a prompt significantly influences the output. I even asked AI to explain prompt engineering in a more detailed way. Here's what it told me:

> AI models don't "think" like humans—they generate text based on probabilities and learned patterns. That means vague or poorly worded prompts can lead to vague or unhelpful answers. Prompt engineering helps you get clearer, more accurate, and more useful results. For example, a **simple prompt** might be: *"Tell me about climate change."* This will give a general overview. A **refined prompt** (better prompt engineering) might be: *"Explain the main causes of climate change*

in a way a high school student could understand, using examples." This is clearer, more specific, and guides the AI to match a particular audience and tone.

While AI can also help us refine our prompts, we still need humans to think through problems, using language to ask AI for help.

In the end, I'm still scared of the implications and applications of AI in our lives. However, I'm trying to lean into the changing landscape of how technology is touching every part of our lives. I'm trying to examine my own defensiveness and apply some of the strategies in this book to my own experience. I'm trying to accept that I will make many mistakes as we all continue to change.

As conversations about artificial intelligence become more widespread, defensiveness around its use often reveals deeper fears about loss of control, bias, and displacement. Whether it's mistrust of AI-generated feedback, fear of surveillance, or resistance to automation, these reactions are rarely just about the technology itself—they tap into long-standing insecurities about power, identity, and societal change. This kind of defensiveness doesn't exist in a vacuum; it thrives in the broader context of an increasingly polarized, digital world where information moves fast, identities are public, and disagreement can feel deeply personal. To move forward—both with technology and with each other—we need strategies that reduce this reactivity and create space for reflection, learning, and collaboration.

STRATEGIES TO REDUCE DEFENSIVENESS IN A POLARIZED, DIGITAL WORLD

One way to help people feel less defensive is called **prebunking**. This strategy works like a vaccine for the brain. If you give someone a small dose of false information—and then show them why it's wrong—they are more prepared to resist bigger lies later. This was first tested by McGuire (1964) and has been used more recently to help people online. Lewandowsky et al. (2017) showed that teaching people how to recognize common tricks used in fake news helped them think more clearly and less emotionally. For example, teaching someone about how AI scams can work may make them less likely to panic when they see a scary headline.

Another solution is creating **safe spaces for disagreement**. This means letting people ask questions or share concerns without fear of being made fun of or punished. In schools and online, people often stay quiet because they're afraid of being judged. Argyris (1990) said that organizations grow more when people feel safe enough to challenge ideas. Online, spaces like Reddit AMAs or forums with strong moderators help people discuss tough topics calmly. For example, a group that feels scared of AI could be invited to a town hall where they can ask experts anything—no question is too small or silly. That kind of safety helps people move from fear to curiosity.

It's also helpful to connect new ideas to values people already care about. This technique is called **moral reframing**. Instead of trying to prove someone wrong, you show how your idea supports something they believe in. Feinberg and Willer (2013) found that if you talk about protecting nature as a way of keeping things "pure" and "clean," more conservative people were open to environmental messages. The same strategy works with AI. If people are worried about job loss, we can talk about how AI can help create *different* jobs, not just take them away.

Finally, people are less defensive when they understand what AI is and feel included in decisions. That's where AI literacy and public participation come in. Floridi et al. (2018) say it's important to make AI tools explainable—meaning people should know how they work and what choices they make. When communities help set the rules for AI, people feel respected and in control. For example, if a school district plans to use AI to track attendance, they could invite parents and students to learn about the system and give feedback. This makes AI something that happens *with* people, not *to* them.

Case Study 5.7 Harold and the Feedback Tool

SCENARIO

Harold is a 62-year-old team manager at a large company. His company starts using an AI tool that gives feedback on leadership style, including areas for improvement. The report says Harold tends to interrupt his team members too much during meetings. Harold feels shocked and embarrassed. He tells his coworkers that "these tools don't understand people" and "this is just a way for the company to get rid of older workers." He avoids talking about the feedback and keeps leading meetings the same way.

ANALYSIS

Harold is showing resistance to AI feedback, driven by defensiveness. Instead of seeing the feedback as a chance to improve, he attacks the tool. He may also feel existential threat—worried that his experience no longer matters. Harold might be reacting not just to the data, but to how the data make him feel about himself. If his company offered a safe space to ask questions and a workshop about how the AI tool works, Harold might feel more open to change. This is where prebunking, safe dialogue, and shared values (e.g., being a strong leader) could help.

Reflective Exercise: Your Feelings About AI

Step 1: Warm-Up—Think About a Reaction

Can you remember a time when you felt upset or confused about a new kind of technology (AI, self-checkouts, smart speakers, etc.)? What happened? How did you feel?

Step 2: Journal Prompt

What story do you believe about that technology? Did your belief come from personal experience, news, movies, or friends? Was your reaction more about fear or facts?

Step 3: Reframe the Story

Write a new version of that story using curiosity instead of fear. Example: "Instead of saying AI will take over everything, I want to learn how it could help people do their jobs better."

Step 4: Share and Discuss

Why do you think people defend themselves against AI or new technology? What would make you feel safer or more confident in using AI tools?

Defensiveness becomes a barrier in the digital age when it prevents truth-seeking, collaboration, and adaptation. In political contexts, it deepens polarization. In AI debates, it clouds critical judgment with fear or ideology. But defensiveness is not destiny. By cultivating self-awareness, designing institutions that value reflection, and promoting respectful public discourse—online and offline—we can move beyond reactivity toward genuine understanding.

MORE IDEAS ON HOW TO USE THIS BOOK

As we conclude, I want to offer some further suggestions on how you might use this book for educational purposes and training in a variety of contexts, including activist and nonprofit groups, classrooms, and workplaces. After reviewing the resources in this guidebook, I encourage you to implement them, modify, and expand upon them for your own purposes. This may include individual growth and learning, and facilitating group cohesiveness and productivity. What follows are some ideas that use the cases of queer rights advocacy and environmental justice groups as examples.

Preparing

Before you begin, it's important to tailor the training to your group's specific needs. For example, if you're working with activists focused on LGBTQ+ rights, prepare examples that touch on defensiveness around sexual identity—such as when someone reacts defensively to questions about their sexuality or gender expression. In environmental groups, defensiveness may arise when discussing personal responsibility for climate change or critiquing practices that harm the planet.

_____

Example

Imagine a group of activists discussing the need for stricter climate policies. Some members who drive gas-powered cars may feel defensive when called out, fearing judgment or exclusion. Recognizing this allows facilitators to frame conversations empathetically, reducing resistance.

_____

Introducing the Concept of Defensiveness

Begin with clear definitions and real-world examples of defensiveness. Explain how people protect themselves emotionally when their beliefs or identities feel threatened. In conversations about sexuality, defensiveness might occur when someone's beliefs about traditional family structures are challenged. With environmental issues, people might become defensive when their shopping habits or choices are questioned.

Example

During a discussion about LGBTQ+ inclusivity, a participant might react defensively to questions about pronoun use because it challenges their previous understanding. Similarly, in an environmental workshop, someone might deny the impact of their plastic use because admitting it feels overwhelming or guilt inducing.

Using Exercises and Activities

Individual Reflection

Ask participants to reflect on moments when they felt defensive about their sexual orientation or environmental habits. This helps connect defensiveness to personal experiences.

Role-Playing

Create scenarios as in a person coming out at work facing subtle defensiveness from a coworker, or an environmental activist debates with a family member resistant to recycling.

Group Discussions

Explore how defensiveness over sexuality or environmental responsibility can hinder advocacy efforts or community building.

Creative Activities

Encourage writing or drawing about feelings triggered by environmental critiques or experiences of exclusion based on sexuality.

Example

In a role-play, one participant might express frustration when a friend dismisses their nonbinary identity, leading to defensive withdrawal or anger. Another might role-play responding to someone defensive about driving a gas car by focusing on shared goals rather than blame.

Applying the Guidebook in Different Settings

Activists
Help LGBTQ+ activists recognize that defensiveness might emerge not just externally but within the community, for example, over differing views on how to approach inclusion. Environmental activists might see defensiveness when discussing sacrifices needed to reduce carbon footprints.

Nonprofit Groups
Nonprofits serving sexual minority youth might address defensiveness when youth feel stigmatized or misunderstood. Environmental nonprofits might help staff manage defensiveness around budget constraints that limit sustainable options.

Classrooms
Students might become defensive when asked to reconsider stereotypes about sexuality or their family's environmental impact. Teachers can use the guidebook to foster openness.

Workplaces
Employees might show defensiveness when company policies require LGBTQ+ inclusion training or green initiatives. Managers can use strategies to ease tension and encourage dialogue.

Example

In a workplace, a manager introduces pronoun sharing but meets defensiveness from some employees. Using the guidebook, the manager facilitates exercises to explore fears and misunderstandings, building empathy and reducing resistance.

Follow-Up and Continued Practice
Encourage participants to keep noticing when defensiveness arises in discussions about sexuality or environmental responsibility. Journaling can include reflecting on moments when they felt defensive about their sexual identity or habits like energy use.

Create peer groups focused on ongoing support around these sensitive topics. Integrate defensiveness awareness into regular training on inclusion and sustainability to normalize growth.

Example

An environmental group forms a monthly circle where members share struggles and defenses related to adopting greener lifestyles, supporting gradual change without judgment. Similarly, an LGBTQ+ youth group uses journaling prompts to explore feelings about coming out and reactions from family or peers.

Here are a few takeaway lessons that I hope you gather from this guidebook:

- Everyone is defensive at times. Defense mechanisms are there to protect us.
- Defensiveness is largely unconscious, outside of our awareness.
- Recognizing and identifying defensiveness is the most important first step in making change.
- It takes practice, time, and a lot of work to learn from our own defensive tendencies, but this can lead to more honest, open, and productive relationships, not only with others, but also with yourself.
- Our emotions drive our thoughts and behaviors.

FINAL THOUGHTS

Defense mechanisms are a cornerstone of psychological understanding, bridging theory and practice across a wide range of disciplines. Your growing awareness of these processes will deepen your empathy. Learning to recognize and work with defenses—first in yourself, then in others—is a vital step in developing your personal and professional identity. Our understanding of defense mechanisms is more than theoretical—it's foundational to our relationships. The ways we protect ourselves can offer deep insights into our inner world, developmental history, and core fears. Recognizing and responding to our defenses is not about dismantling them prematurely, but about holding space for their meaning in order to learn from them.

WHERE TO GO FROM HERE

If this book has sparked your curiosity, consider exploring related areas such as attachment theory, trauma-informed therapy, mindfulness practices, or emotion regulation strategies. Each offers complementary insights into how we manage internal conflict and relate to the world around us. Clinical work, journaling, or even simply observing your own reactions during moments of stress can serve as powerful tools for continued discovery. Notice how you react in moments of discomfort: Do you withdraw, lash out, rationalize, or numb out? Each response holds a clue. The more we can name our defenses, the more empowered we become to do something about them.

FUTURE DIRECTIONS

Research on defense mechanisms is expanding, thanks in part to advances in neuropsychology, brain imaging, and integrative therapeutic models. There is increasing interest in how culture, environment, and developmental history shape defensive patterns. Furthermore, AI and machine learning may soon help map psychological defenses in ways never before possible, offering new tools for therapists and researchers alike. The field is moving toward greater integration and interdisciplinarity: psychoanalysis meets neuroscience; cognitive science meets trauma theory. Online platforms, apps, and communities are making psychological tools more accessible than ever. Even as our technologies expand, they are just tools to assist with an inherently personal, human experience. As our culture becomes more emotionally aware, there is a growing interest in mental health, trauma healing, and emotional intelligence. In the coming years, we can expect a greater emphasis on preventative mental healthcare and self-understanding.

As we learn to be more comfortable in the state of the 8 Cs of open heartedness: calmness, curiosity, clarity, compassion, confidence, courage, creativity, and connectedness (Schwartz & Sweezy, 2020), we learn that we often arrive at the end of an exploration with more questions than answers. By continuing to ask more and more questions, you'll be engaging in the very work that makes emotional growth possible. You, the reader, are also witness to my own journey in defensiveness, as this guidebook is the culmination of decades of personal and professional study. I have come to appreciate the nuance, sophistication, and power of defense mechanisms. I have felt relief in knowing how to understand and label my own experiences. I can sometimes feel a sense of agency or accomplishment when I can now make meaning out of a confusing or painful situation. Often I feel sadness and despair as I observe myself respond with behaviors that are part of old, repeated patterns that I wish I could change. I continue to be fascinated at the ways that power and social structures cultivate internal experiences that we tend to believe are personal and private, but are really reflections of larger social and political structures. I have witnessed myself and my students feel empowered, encouraged, motivated and inspired to learn more, apply our knowledge and skills, and just keep going. Defense mechanisms may always be part of the human experience, but awareness empowers us to use them more wisely—and, when needed, to grow beyond them.

References

Affleck, G., & Tennen, H. (1996). Construing benefits from adversity: Adaptational significance and dispositional underpinnings. *Journal of Personality, 64*, 899–922.

Allan, C. A. (1995). Alcohol problems and anxiety disorders – A critical review. *Alcohol and Alcoholism, 30*(2), 145–151.

Allport, G. W., Clark, K., & Pettigrew, T. (1954). *The nature of prejudice.* Addison-Wesley Publishing Company.

Amodeo, J. (2016, September 22). *4 hidden ways shame operates.* https://psychcentral.com/blog/4-hidden-ways-shame-operates#1

Applebaum, B. (2010). *Being white, being good: White complicity, white moral responsibility, and social justice pedagogy.* Lexington Books.

Applewhite, A. (2019). *This chair rocks: A manifesto against ageism.* Celadon Books.

Argyris, C. (1990). *Overcoming organizational defenses: Facilitating organizational learning.* Allyn & Bacon.

Aronson, E. (1969). A theory of cognitive dissonance: A current perspective. *Advances in Experimental Social Psychology, 4*, 1–34.

Asadi, F., Pirkalani, R. K., & Mehrinezhad, S. A. (2022). The role of emotional self-regulation strategies, defense mechanisms and integrative self-knowledge in predicting quality of interpersonal relationships. *Journal of Modern Psychological Researches, 17*(67), 1–11. https://doi.org/10.22034/JMPR.2022.15314

Assari, S. (2017, June 30). *Why poverty is not a personal choice, but a reflection of society.* The Conversation. https://theconversation.com/why-poverty-is-not-a-personal-choice-but-a-reflection-of-society-79552

Transforming Defensiveness: A Guidebook for Rewriting Our Stories & Reclaiming Connection, First Edition. Andrea L. Dottolo.
© 2026 John Wiley & Sons, Inc. All rights reserved, including rights for text and data mining and training of artificial intelligence technologies or similar technologies.
Published 2026 by John Wiley & Sons, Inc.

Asquith, J. L., & Bristow, D. N. (2000). To catch a thief: A pedagogical study of retail shoplifting. *Journal of Education for Business, 75*(5), 271–277.

Baker, W. H. (1980). Defensiveness in communication: Its causes, effects, and cures. *The Journal of Business Communication (1973), 17*(3), 33–43. https://doi.org/10.1177/002194368001700304

Bakshy, E., Messing, S., & Adamic, L. A. (2015). Exposure to ideologically diverse news and opinion on Facebook. *Science, 348*(6239), 1130–1132.

Bandura, A. (1999). Moral disengagement in the perpetration of inhumanities. *Personality and Social Psychology Review, 3*(3), 193–209. https://doi.org/10.1207/s15327957pspr0303_3

Bandura, A., & Walters, R. H. (1977). *Social learning theory* (Vol. 1, pp. 141–154). Prentice Hall.

Banks, I. (2011). Control or repression: Contrasting a prisoner of war camp and a work camp from World War Two. In A. Myers & G. Moshenska (Eds.), *Archaeologies of internment. One world archaeology.* Springer. https://doi.org/10.1007/978-1-4419-9666-4_7

Barber, B. K., Olsen, J. E., & Shagle, S. C. (1994). Associations between parental psychological and behavioral control and youth internalized and externalized behaviors. *Child Development, 65*(4), 1120–1136.

Barry, P. G., & Welsh, M. (2007). The BrainWise curriculum: Neurocognitive development intervention program. In D. Romer & E. Walker (Eds.), *Adolescent psychopathology and the developing brain: Integrating brain and prevention science* (pp. 420–440). Oxford University Press.

Baumeister, R. F., Stillwell, A. M., & Heatherton, T. F. (1994). Guilt: An interpersonal approach. *Psychological Bulletin, 115*(2), 243–267. https://doi.org/10.1037/0033-2909.115.2.243

Bennis, W., Goleman, D., & O'Toole, J. (2008). *Transparency: How leaders create a culture of candor.* John Wiley & Sons.

Berenbaum, S. A., & Beltz, A. M. (2016). How early hormones shape gender development. *Current Opinion in Behavioral Sciences, 7,* 53–60. https://doi.org/10.1016/j.cobeha.2015.11.011

Berger, B. G. (1994). Coping with stress: The effectiveness of exercise and other techniques. *Quest, 46*(1), 100–119.

Bigler, R. S. (1999). The use of multicultural curricula and materials to counter racism in children. *Journal of Social Issues, 55*(4), 687–705.

Bond, M. (2004). Empirical studies of defense style: Relationships with psychopathology and change. *Harvard Review of Psychiatry, 12*(5), 263–278. https://doi.org/10.1080/10673220490910865

Börsch-Supan, A. (2013). Myths, scientific evidence and economic policy in an aging world. *The Journal of the Economics of Ageing, 1–2*, 3–15. https://doi.org/10.1016/j.jeoa.2013.06.001

Brach, T. (2020). *Radical compassion: Learning to love yourself and your world with the practice of RAIN*. Penguin.

Bracket, M., & Stern, R. (2024, March). *A brief history of emotional intelligence*. Psychology Today.

Bradshaw, J. (2005). *Healing the shame that binds you*. Health Communications, Inc.

Branscombe, N. R., Ellemers, N., Spears, R., & Doosje, B. (1999). The context and content of social identity threat. In N. Ellemers, R. Spears, & B. Doosje (Eds.), *Social identity: Context, commitment, content* (pp. 35–58). Blackwell Science.

Brewer, M. B. (1979). In-group bias in the minimal intergroup situation: A cognitive-motivational analysis. *Psychological Bulletin, 86*(2), 307–324. https://doi.org/10.1037/0033-2909.86.2.307

Brizendine, L. (2006). *The female brain*. Morgan Road Books.

Brookings Institution. (2022). *Artificial intelligence and public trust: Challenges and opportunities*. Brookings Institution. https://www.brookings.edu/

Brown, B. (2012). *Daring greatly: How the courage to be vulnerable transforms the way we live, love, parent, and lead*. Penguin Group Inc.

Brown, B. (2018). *Dare to lead: Brave work. Tough conversations. Whole hearts.* Random House.

Brown, R., & Gerbarg, P. L. (2012). *The healing power of the breath: Simple techniques to reduce stress and anxiety, enhance concentration, and balance your emotions*. Shambhala Publications.

Bugental, J. F., & Bugental, E. K. (1984). A fate worse than death: The fear of changing. *Psychotherapy: Theory, Research, Practice, Training, 21*(4), 543–549. https://doi.org/10.1037/h0086000

Buller, D. B., & Burgoon, J. K. (1996). Interpersonal deception theory. *Communication Theory, 6*(3), 203–242.

Burke, K. (2016). *Christians under covers: Evangelicals and sexual pleasure on the internet*. University of California Press.

Burton, R., & Sheron, N. (2018). No level of alcohol consumption improves health. *The Lancet, 392*, 987–988.

Buttelmann, D., & Bohm, R. (2014). The ontogeny of the motivation that underlies in-group bias. *Psychological Science, 25*(4), 921–927. https://doi.org/10.1177/0956797613516802

Buunk, B. P., & Dijkstra, P. (2001). Rationalizations and defensive attributions for high-risk sex among heterosexuals. *Patient Education and Counseling, 45*(2), 127–132. https://doi.org/10.1016/S0738-3991(01)00114-8

Cambridge Dictionary. (2017). *Bias.* Cambridge University Press. Retrieved from http://dictionary.cambridge.org/dictionary/english/bi

Candilis, P. J. (2023). Honoring DEI requires a new ethic and a new science. *The Journal of the American Academy of Psychiatry and the Law, 51*(4), 494–499.

Cannon, W. B. (1929). *Bodily changes in pain, hunger, fear, and rage.* Appleton.

Caporaso, J. A., & Jupille, J. (Eds.). (2022). Definitions of institutions. In *Theories of institutions* (pp. 159–164). Cambridge University Press. https://doi.org/10.1017/9781139034142.007, ISBN 978-0-521-87929-3, S2CID 245805736

Cherry, M. (2019). Gendered failures in extrinsic emotional regulation; Or, why telling a woman to "relax" or a young boy to "stop crying like a girl" is not a good idea. *Philosophical Topics, 47*(2), 95–112. https://www.jstor.org/stable/26948108

Chitty, C. (2009). *Eugenics, race and intelligence in education.* A&C Black.

Chrisler, J. C. (2007). The subtleties of meaning: Still arguing after all these years. *Feminism & Psychology, 17*(4), 442–446. https://doi.org/10.1177/0959353507084323

Claney, C. (2024, November 21). *Projection as a defense mechanism: Understanding the psychology behind it.* Relational Psych. https://www.relationalpsych.group/articles/projection-as-a-defense-mechanism-understanding-the-psychology-behind-it

Clarke, A., Evans, A. B., Gabriel, R. A., & Milam, A. J. (2022). Race-and ethnicity-based clinical algorithms: Implications for perioperative medicine. *Anesthesia and Analgesia, 10,* 1213.

Clayton, I. (2025). *Fawning: Why the need to please makes us lose ourselves--and how to find our way back.* G. P. Putnam's Sons.

Cole, E. R., & Stewart, A. J. (1996). Meanings of political participation among Black and White Women: Political identity and social responsibility. *Journal of Personality and Social Psychology, 71,* 130–140.

Collins, P. H. (1990). *Black feminist thought: Knowledge, consciousness, and the politics of empowerment.* Harper Collins.

Collins, R. (1996). For better or worse: The impact of upward social comparison on self-evaluations. *Psychological Bulletin, 119*(1), 51–69.

Comas-Díaz, L., Hall, G. N., & Neville, H. A. (2019). Racial trauma: Theory, research, and healing: Introduction to the special issue. *American Psychologist, 74*(1), 1.

Comer, R. J. (2010). *Abnormal psychology* (7th ed.). Worth.

Cornell, D. (2024). *17 confirmation bias examples.* www.helpfulprofessor.com

Corrigan, R. (2006). Making meaning of Megan's law. *Law & Social Inquiry, 31,* 267–312. https://doi.org/10.1111/j.1747-4469.2006.00012.x

Coulter, R. W. S., Mair, C., Miller, E., Blosnich, J. R., Matthews, D. D., & McCauley, H. L. (2017). Prevalence of past-year sexual assault victimization among undergraduate students: Exploring differences by and intersections of gender identity, sexual identity, and race/ethnicity. *Prevention Science, 18,* 726–736.

Cozzarelli, C., Wilkinson, A. V., & Tagler, M. J. (2001). Attitudes toward the poor and attributions for poverty. *Journal of Social Issues, 57*(2), 207–227.

Cramer, P. (1991). *The development of defense mechanisms.* Springer. https://doi.org/10.1007/978-1-4613-9025-1_12

Cramer, P. (1998). Coping and defense mechanisms: What's the difference? *Journal of Personality, 66*(6), 919–946.

Cramer, P. (2000). Defense mechanisms in psychology today: Further processes for adaptation. *American Psychologist, 55*(6), 637–646. https://doi.org/10.1037//0003-066x.55.6.637

Cramer, P. (2006). *Protecting the self: Defense mechanisms in action.* Guilford Press.

Cramer, P. (2015). Understanding defense mechanisms. *Psychodynamic Psychiatry, 43*(4), 523–552. https://doi.org/10.1521/pdps.2015.43.4.523

Crenshaw, K., Gotanda, N., Peller, G., & Thomas, K. (Eds.). (1995). *Critical race theory: The key writings that formed the movement.* The New Press.

Croyle, R. T., Sun, Y., & Louie, D. H. (1993). Psychological minimization of cholesterol test results: Moderators of appraisal in college students and community residents. *Health Psychology, 12*(6), 503–507.

Curzuer, H. J. (2012). *Aristotle & the Virtues.* Oxford University Press.

David, E. J. R., & Derthick, A. O. (2017). *The psychology of oppression.* Springer Publishing Company.

David, D. H., & Lyons-Ruth, K. (2005). Differential attachment responses of male and female infants to frightening maternal behavior: Tend or befriend versus fight or flight? *Infant Mental Health Journal, 26*(1), 1–18. https://doi.org/10.1002/imhj.20033

David, E. J. R., Schroeder, T. M., & Fernandez, J. (2019). Internalized racism: A systematic review of the psychological literature on racism's most insidious consequence. *Journal of Social Issues, 75*(4), 1057–1086.

Deci, E. L., & Ryan, R. M. (2013). *Intrinsic motivation and self-determination in human behavior.* Springer Science & Business Media.

Della Selva, P. C. (2018). *Intensive short-term dynamic psychotherapy: Theory and technique.* Routledge.

DeMala-Moran, C. L. (2018). The 7 C's of well-being. In K. S. Trotter & J. N. Baggerly (Eds.), *Equine-assisted mental health interventions* (pp. 177–183). Routledge.

DeNisco, A. (2016). *Myth busted: Older workers are just as tech-savvy as younger ones, says new survey*. TechRepublic. Retrieved January 17, 2017, from http://www.techrepublic.com/article/myth-busted-older-workers-are-just-as-tech-savvy-as-younger-ones-says-new-survey/

Dixon, A. R., & Telles, E. E. (2017). Skin color and colorism: Global research, concepts, and measurement. *Annual Review of Sociology, 43*(1), 405–424.

Dixon, L. J., Witcraft, S. M., & Schadegg, M. J. (2023). COVID-19 anxiety and mental health among university students in the early phases of the U.S. pandemic. *Journal of American College Health, 71*(4), 1152–1160.

Dorahy, M. J. (2017). Shame as a compromise for humiliation and rage in the internal representation of abuse by loved ones: Processes, motivations, and the role of dissociation. *Journal of Trauma & Dissociation, 18*(3), 383–396. https://doi.org/10.1080/15299732.2017.1295422

Dorpat, T. (1985). *Denial and defense in the therapeutic situation*. Jason Aronson Inc.

Dottolo, A.L. (2019). Overcoming Student Defensiveness in Social Psychology Courses: A Collaborative Workshop for Discussing Privilege and Prejudice. In J. Mena & K. Quina (Eds.), Integrating multiculturalism and intersectionality into the psychology curriculum, (pp. 257–68). Washington, DC: American Psychological Association.

Dottolo, A. L., & Stewart, A. J. (2008). "Don't ever forget now, you're a Black man in America": Intersections of race, class and gender in encounters with the police. *Sex Roles, 59*, 350–364. https://doi.org/10.1007/s11199-007-9387-x

Dunn, K., & Nelson, J. K. (2011). Challenging the public denial of racism for a deeper multiculturalism. *Journal of Intercultural Studies, 32*(6), 587–602. https://doi.org/10.1080/07256868.2011.618105

Elliott, J. (2018). 10 It's all about ignorance: Reflections from the Blue-eyed/Brown-eyed exercise. In *The Cambridge handbook of the psychology of prejudice: Concise student edition* (p. 253). Cambridge University Press.

Ellis, W. E., & Zarbatany, L. (2017). Understanding processes of peer clique influence in late childhood and early adolescence. *Child Development Perspectives, 11*(4), 227–232.

Eustaquio, P. C., Olansky, E., Lee, K., Marcus, R., & Cha, S. (2025). The association between sexual violence and suicidal ideation among transgender women and the role of gender-affirming healthcare providers in seven urban areas in the United States, 2019 to 2020. *Journal of Interpersonal Violence*, *40*(5–6), 1090–1111.

Evans, N. J., & Washington, J. (2010). Becoming an ally: A new examination. In M. Adams, W. J. Blumenfeld, C. R. Castañeda, H. W. Hackman, M. L. Peters, & X. Zúñiga (Eds.), *Readings for diversity and social justice* (Vol. 2, pp. 413–421).

Fee, R. L., & Tangney, J. P. (2000). Procrastination: A means of avoiding shame or guilt? *Journal of Social Behavior & Personality*, *15*(5), 167.

Ferriss, A. L. (2006). Social structure and child poverty. *Social Indicators Research*, *78*, 453–472.

Feinberg, M., & Willer, R. (2013). The moral roots of environmental attitudes. *Psychological Science*, *24*(1), 56–62.

Festinger, L. (1954). A theory of social comparison processes. *Human Relations*, *7*(2), 117–140.

Fillmore, K. M., Kerr, W. C., Stockwell, T., Chikritzhs, T., & Bostrom, A. (2006). Moderate alcohol use and reduced mortality risk: Systematic error in prospective studies. *Addiction Research and Theory*, *14*, 101–132.

Fleming, S. M., Thomas, C. L., & Dolan, R. J. (2010). Overcoming status quo bias in the human brain. *Biological Sciences*, *107*(13), 6005–6009.

Floridi, L., Cowls, J., Beltrametti, M., Chatila, R., Chazerand, P., Dignum, V., Luetge, C., Madelin, R., Pagallo, U., Rossi, F., Schafer, B., Valcke, P., & Vayena, E. (2018). AI4People—An ethical framework for a good AI society: Opportunities, risks, principles, and recommendations. *Minds and Machines*, *28*(4), 689–707.

Ford, T. E., & Ferguson, M. A. (2004). Social consequences of disparagement humor: A prejudiced norm theory. *Personality and Social Psychology Review*, *8*(1), 79–94.

Foster, C. A., & Ortiz, S. M. (2017). Vaccines, autism, and the promotion of irrelevant research. In K. Frazier & B. Radford (Eds.), *Unreason: Best of skeptical inquirer* (Vol. 7, pp. 269–277). Prometheus Books.

Fouts, H. N., Hewlett, B. S., & Lamb, M. E. (2012). A biocultural approach to breastfeeding interactions in Central Africa. *American Anthropologist*, *114*(1), 123–136.

Freud, A. (1918). Triebe und Triebschicksale im Lichte verschiedener Abwehrleistungen. [Drives and their vicissitudes in the light of different defense performances]. *Internationale Zeitschrift für Psychoanalyse*, *4*, 258–268.

Freud, A. (1963). The concept of developmental lines. *The Psychoanalytic Study of the Child*, *18*(1), 245–265.

Freud, A. (1966). *The ego and the mechanisms of defense* (Rev. ed.). International Universities Press. (Original work published 1936)

Freud, S. (1894). The neuro-psychoses of defence. In S. J. London (Ed.), *The standard edition of the complete psychology works of Sigmund Freud* (Vol. 3, pp. 45–61). Hogarth Press.

Freud, S. (1923). *Das Ich und das Es*. Internationaler Psychoanalytischer Verlag.

Freud, S. (1926). *The ego and the Id*. Hogarth Press.

Freud, S. (1953). *Three essays on the theory of sexuality* (J. Strachey, Trans.). In J. Strachey (Ed.), *The standard edition of the complete psychological works of Sigmund Freud* (Vol. 7, pp. 123–245). Hogarth Press. (Original work published 1905)

Furnham, A. (2003). Belief in a just world: Research progress over the past decade. *Personality and Individual Differences, 34*(5), 795–817.

Galanis, C. R., & King, D. L. (2025). Stigma and other public perceptions of recreational gaming and gaming disorder: A large-scale qualitative analysis. *Computers in Human Behavior Reports, 17*, 100581.

Gallucci, G. M. (2000). *Plato and Freud: Statesmen of the soul*. Xlibris Corporation.

Gaston, H. K. (2023). *How to survive a toxic boss*. Dorrance Publishing.

Gay, C., & Tate, K. (1998). Doubly bound: The impact of gender and race on the politics of Black women. *Political Psychology, 19*(1), 169–184.

GBD Alcohol Collaborators. (2018). Alcohol use and burden for 195 countries and territories, 1990-2016: A systematic analysis for the Global Burden of Disease Study 2016. *Lancet, 392*, 1015–1035.

Gibb, J. (1961). Defensive communication. *Journal of Communication, 11*(3), 141–148.

Gibbons, F. X., & Gerrard, M. (1989). Effects of upward and downward social comparison on mood states. *Journal of Social and Clinical Psychology, 8*(1), 14–31. https://doi.org/10.1521/jscp.1989.8.1.14

Gibson, L. C. (2015). *Adult children of emotionally immature parents: How to heal from distant, rejecting, or self-involved parents*. New Harbinger Publications.

Giddings, P. (1984). *When and where I enter*. Bantam.

Glick, P. (2005). Choice of scapegoats. In J. F. Dovidio, P. Glick, & L. A. Rudman (Eds.), *On the nature of prejudice: Fifty years after Allport* (pp. 244–261). Blackwell Publishing Ltd.

Goleman, D. (2005). *Emotional intelligence: Why it can matter more than IQ*. Bantam Books.

Goodman, S., & Carr, P. (2017). The just world hypothesis as an argumentative resource in debates about unemployment benefits. *Journal of Community & Applied Social Psychology, 27*(4), 312–323.

Goodnough, A. (2012, January 26). Student faces town's wrath in protest against a prayer. *The New York Times.* https://www.nytimes.com/2012/01/27/us/rhode-island-city-enraged-over-school-prayer-lawsuit.html

Gottman, J. M., & Silver, N. (1999). *The seven principles for making marriage work.* Crown Publishing Group.

Griffin, S. (1971). Rape: The all-American crime. *Ramparts, 10*(3), 26–35.

Gruenert, S., & Whitaker, T. (2019). *Committing to the culture: How leaders can create and sustain positive schools.* ASCD.

Hamer, D. (2011). *The science of desire: The search for the gay gene and the biology of behavior.* Simon & Schuster.

Hammond, Z. (2014). *Culturally responsive teaching & the brain: Promoting authentic engagement and rigor among culturally and linguistically diverse students.* Corwin.

Harding, K. (2015). *Asking for it: The alarming rise of rape culture--and what we can do about it.* Da Capo Lifelong Books.

Harmon-Jones, E., & Mills, J. (2019). An introduction to cognitive dissonance theory and an overview of current perspectives on the theory. In E. Harmon-Jones (Ed.), *Cognitive dissonance: Reexamining a pivotal theory in psychology* (2nd ed., pp. 3–24). American Psychological Association. https://doi.org/10.1037/0000135-001

Harro, B. (2000). The cycle of liberation. In M. Adams, W. Blumenfeld, R. Castaneda, H. Hackman, M. L. Peters, & X. Zuniga (Eds.), *Readings for Diversity and Social Justice.* Routledge.

Hastings, M., Northman, L., & Tangney, J. (2002). Shame, guilt, and suicide. In T. E. Joiner & M. D. Rudd (Eds.), *Suicide science: Expanding the boundaries* (pp. 67–79). Springer.

Hawkins, E. (2025, January 5). *What happened to Matthew Shepard's killers, Aaron McKinney and Russell Henderson?* Oxygen True Crime. https://www.oxygen.com/uncovered-killed-by-hate/crime-news/matthew-shepards-killers-russell-henderson-aaron-mckinney-hate-crime

Hayes, A. F., Glynn, C. J., & Shanahan, J. (2005). Willingness to self-censor: A construct and measurement tool for public opinion research. *The International Journal of Public Opinion Research, 17*(3), 298–323.

Haynes, S. R. (2002). *Noah's curse: The biblical justification of American slavery.* Oxford University Press.

Hendel, H. J. (2018). *It's not always depression: Working the change triangle to listen to the body, discover core emotions, and connect to your authentic self*. Random House.

Herman, J. L. (2015). *Trauma and recovery: The aftermath of violence--from domestic abuse to political terror*. Hachette UK.

Hewlett, B. S., & Winn, S. (2014). Allomaternal nursing in humans. *Current Anthropology*, *55*(2), 200–229.

Higgs, R. (2006). Fear: The foundation of every government's power. *The Independent Review*, *10*(3), 447–466.

Hitchcock, J. (1984). The sinking feeling. *The Psychoanalytic Study of the Child*, *39*(1), 321–329. https://doi.org/10.1080/00797308.1984.11823432

Hofstede, G. (1980). *Culture's consequences: International differences in work-related values*. Sage.

hooks, bell. (1989). *Talking back*. South End Press.

House, J. S. (1981). Social structure and personality. In M. Rosenberg & R. H. Turner (Eds.), *Social psychology: Sociological perspectives* (pp. 525–561). Basic Books.

Hunter, A. G., & Sellers, S. L. (1998). Feminist attitudes among African American women and men. *Gender & Society*, *12*(1), 81–99.

Islam, M. S., Sarkar, T., Khan, S. H., Kamal, A. M., Hasan, S. M. M., Kabir, A., Yeasmin, D., Islam, M. A., Chowdhury, K. I. A., Anwar, K. S., Chughtai, A. A., & Seale, H. (2020). COVID-19-related infodemic and its impact on public health: A global social media analysis. *The American Journal of Tropical Medicine and Hygiene*, *103*(4), 1621–1629. https://doi.org/10.4269/ajtmh.20-0812

Jhally, S., Earp, J., & Young, J. T. (Eds.). (2017). *Advertising at the Edge of the Apocalypse*. Media Education Foundation.

Jhangiani, R., & Tarry, H. (2022). *Principles of social psychology - 1st International H5P edition*. https://opentextbc.ca/socialpsychology/

Johnson, A. G. (1980). On the prevalence of rape in the United States. *Signs: Journal of Women in Culture and Society*, *6*(1), 136–146.

Kan, F. P., Raoofi, S., Rafiei, S., Khani, S., Hosseinifard, H., Tajik, F., Raoofi, N., Ahmadi, S., Aghalou, S., Torabi, F., Dehnad, A., Rezaei, S., Hosseinipalangi, Z., & Ghashghaee, A. (2021). A systematic review of the prevalence of anxiety among the general population during the COVID-19 pandemic. *Journal of Affective Disorders*, *293*, 391–398. https://www.sciencedirect.com/science/article/pii/S0165032721006595

Kaplan, H. (2012). Belief in a just world, religiosity and victim blaming. *Archive for the Psychology of Religion*, *34*(3), 397–409. https://doi.org/10.1163/15736121-12341246

Keller, H., Abels, M., Lamm, B., Yovsi, R. D., Voelker, S., & Lakhani, A. (2005). Ecocultural effects on early infant care: A study in Cameroon, India and Germany. *Ethos, 33*, 512–541. https://doi.org/10.1525/eth.2005.33.4.512

Kemp, J., Milne, R., & Reay, D. S. (2010). Sceptics and deniers of climate change not to be confused. *Nature, 464*, 673.

Kilbourne, J. (2000). *Can't buy my love: How advertising changes the way we think and feel*. Simon and Schuster.

Kilpatrick, D. G., Resnick, H. S., Saunders, B. E., & Best, C. L. (1998). Rape, other violence against women, and posttraumatic stress disorder. In B. P. Dohrenwend (Ed.), *Adversity, stress, and psychopathology* (pp. 161–176). Oxford University Press.

Kim, S., Thibodeau, R., & Jorgensen, R. S. (2011). Shame, guilt, and depressive symptoms: A meta-analytic review. *Psychological Bulletin, 137*(1), 68–96.

King, D. K. (1997). Multiple jeopardy, multiple consciousness: The context of a black feminist ideology. In D. T. Meyers (Ed.), *Feminist social thought: A reader* (pp. 220–242). Routledge.

King, M. (1975). Oppression and power: The unique status of Black women in the American political system. *Social Science Quarterly, 56*, 117–128.

Kirmayer, L. J., & Looper, K. J. (1998). Somatization and psychologization: Understanding cultural idioms of distress. In S. Okpaku (Ed.), *Culture and psychotherapy: A guide to clinical practice* (pp. 213–236). American Psychiatric Association Press.

Kitzinger, C. (1987). *The social construction of Lesbianism*. Sage Productions.

Knight, J. (1992). *Institutions and social conflict* (pp. 1–2). Cambridge University Press. ISBN 978-0-511-52817-0. OCLC 1127523562

Kolb, D. A. (2014). *Experiential learning: Experience as the source of learning and development*. FT Press.

Kramer, M. D., Krueger, R. F., & Hicks, B. M. (2008). The role of internalizing and externalizing liability. factors in accounting for gender differences in the prevalence of common psychopathological syndromes. *Psychological Medicine, 38*(1), 51–61. https://doi.org/10.1017/S0033291707001572

Krahé, B. (1999). Repression and coping with the threat of rape. *European Journal of Personality, 13*(1), 15–26.

Kraus, M. W., Torrez, B., & Hollie, L. (2022). How narratives of racial progress create barriers to diversity, equity, and inclusion in organizations. *Current Opinion in Psychology, 43*, 108–113.

Lazarus, R. S., & Folkman, S. (1984). *Stress, appraisal, and coping.* Springer.

Lee, J., Jeong, H. J., & Kim, S. (2021). Stress, anxiety, and depression among undergraduate students during the COVID-19 pandemic and their use of mental health services. *Innovative Higher Education, 46,* 519–538. https://doi.org/10.1007/s10755-021-09552-y

Lerner, M. J. (1965). Evaluation of performance as a function of performer's reward and attractiveness. *Journal of Personality and Social Psychology, 1,* 355–360.

Lerner, M. J., & Miller, D. T. (1978). Just world research and the attribution process: Looking back and ahead. *Psychological Bulletin, 85*(5), 1030–1051. https://doi.org/10.1037/0033-2909.85.5.1030

Levine, P. A. (1997). *Waking the tiger: Healing trauma: The innate capacity to transform overwhelming experiences.* North Atlantic Books.

Levinson, B. (Director). (1997). *Wag the dog [Film].* 20th Century Studios.

Levy, B. R. (2017). Age-stereotype paradox: Opportunity for social change. *The Gerontologist, 57*(2), S118–S126. https://doi.org/10.1093/geront/gnx059

Lewandowsky, S., Ecker, U. K., & Cook, J. (2017). Beyond misinformation: Understanding and coping with the "post-truth" era. *Journal of Applied Research in Memory and Cognition, 6*(4), 353–369.

Lindsay-Hartz, J. (1984). Contrasting experiences of shame and guilt. *The American Behavioral Scientist, 27*(6), 689–704.

Lindstrom, M. (2011). *Brandwashed: Tricks companies use to manipulate our minds and persuade us to buy.* Crown Currency.

Lines, D. (2007). *The bullies: Understanding bullies and bullying.* Jessica Kingsley Publishers.

Ling, R. (2020). Confirmation bias in the era of mobile news consumption: The social and psychological dimensions. *Digital Journalism, 8,* 596–604.

Lips, H. M. (2018). *Gender: The basics.* Routledge.

Liu, A. (2011). Unraveling the myth of meritocracy within the context of US higher education. *Higher Education, 62,* 383–397.

Martin, R. A., Puhlik-Doris, P., Larsen, G., Gray, J., & Weir, K. (2003). Individual differences in uses of humor and their relation to psychological well-being: Development of the Humor Styles Questionnaire. *Journal of Research in Personality, 37*(1), 48–75. https://doi.org/10.1016/S0092-6566(02)00534-2

Mason, S. E., Kuntz, C. V., & Mcgill, C. M. (2015). Oldsters and Ngrams: Age stereotypes across time. *Psychological Reports: Sociocultural Issues in Psychology, 116,* 324–329. https://doi.org/10.2466/17.10.PR0.116k17w6

Matias, C. E. (2018). Before cultural competence: A therapy session on exploring the latent and overt emotionalities of whiteness. In S. S. Poulsen

& B. Allan (Eds.), *Cross-cultural responsiveness & systemic therapy* (pp. 21–39). Springer.

McAdams, D. P., & Janis, L. (2004). Narrative identity and narrative therapy. In L. E. Angus & J. McLeod (Eds.), *The handbook of narrative and psychotherapy: Practice, theory, and research* (pp. 159–173). Sage Publications, Inc. https://doi.org/10.4135/9781412973496.d13

McCarty, R. (2016). The fight-or-flight response: A cornerstone of stress research. In G. Fink (Ed.), *Stress: Concepts, cognition, emotion and behavior* (pp. 33–37). Academic Press.

McCoy, K. (2024). *Why you should expand your emotional vocabulary.* Psychology Today.

McEwen, C. A., & McEwen, B. S. (2017). Social structure, adversity, toxic stress, and intergenerational poverty: An early childhood model. *Annual Review of Sociology, 43*(1), 445–472.

McGuire, W. J. (1964). Inducing resistance to persuasion: Some contemporary approaches. *Advances in Experimental Social Psychology, 1*, 192–229.

McLeod, S. (2023). *Stereotypes in psychology: Definition & examples.* Simply Psychology. https://www.simplypsychology.org/katz-braly.html

Midura, D. W., & Glover, D. R. (2005). *Essentials of team building: Principles and practices.* Human Kinetics.

Miller, B. L. (2020). Science denial and COVID conspiracy theories: Potential neurological mechanisms and possible responses. *JAMA, 324*(22), 2255–2256. https://doi.org/10.1001/jama.2020.21332

Miller, A. E., & Josephs, L. (2009). Whiteness as pathological narcissism. *Contemporary Psychoanalysis, 45*(1), 93–119. https://doi.org/10.1080/00107530.2009.10745989

Mirzoeff, N. (2016). The murder of Michael Brown: Reading the Ferguson grand jury transcript. *Social Text, 34*(1), 49–71.

Modgil, S., Singh, R. K., Gupta, S., & Dennehy, D. (2024). A confirmation bias view on social media induced polarisation during Covid-19. *Information Systems Frontiers, 26*, 417–441.

Molenberghs, P. (2013). The neuroscience of in-group bias. *Neuroscience & Biobehavioral Reviews, 37*(8), 1530–1536.

Moreau, S. (2010). What is discrimination? *Philosophy & Public Affairs, 38*(2), 143–179.

Moses, T. D. S., Daniel, E. O., Gatka-al, Z. G., Lubang, W. S., Bello, A. M., Clement, E. G., ... Avwerhota, M. (2021). Attitudes and community perspectives on male involvement in breastfeeding, in Juba, South Sudan. *European Journal of Preventive Medicine, 9*(6), 149–156. doi:10.1080/02699930701822272

Muller, D., & Fayant, M. (2010). On being exposed to superior others: Consequences of self-threatening upward social comparisons. *Social and Personality Psychology Compass, 4*(8), 621–634. https://doi.org/10.1111/j.1751-9004.2010

Murray, J. (2008). *One flesh, two sexes, three genders?* University of Pennsylvania Press.

Naimi, T. S., Stockwell, T., Zhao, J., Xuan, Z., Dangardt, F., Saitz, R., Liang, W., & Chikritzhs, T. (2017). Selection biases in observational studies affect associations between 'moderate' alcohol consumption and mortality. *Addiction, 112*, 207–214.

Napoli, M. (2011). React or respond: A guide to apply mindfulness for families and therapists. *Families in Society, 92*(1), 28–32.

Ni, Y., & Jia, F. (2023). Promoting positive social interactions: Recommendation for a post-pandemic school-based intervention for social anxiety. *Children (Basel), 10*, 491.

Nichols, M. P., & Straus, M. B. (2021). *Lost art of listening.* Guilford Publications.

Nicholson, S., & Domoney-Lyttle, Z. (2020). Women and gender in the Bible and the Biblical World: Editorial introduction. *Open Theology, 6*(1), 706–710. https://doi.org/10.1515/opth-2020-0143

Noor, M., Shnabel, N., Halabi, S., & Nadler, A. (2008). When suffering begets suffering: The psychology of competitive victimhood between adversarial groups in violent conflicts. *Personality and Social Psychology Review, 12*(4), 280–306. https://doi.org/10.1177/1088868308319225

North, D. C. (1991). Institutions. *Journal of Economic Perspectives, 5*(1), 97–112. https://doi.org/10.1257/jep.5.1.97. ISSN 0895-3309

Nortje, A. (2020). *Social comparison theory & 12 real-life examples.* Retrieved September 22, 2024, from https://positivepsychology.com/social-comparison/

Nye, J. S., Zelikow, P. D., & King, D. C. (Eds.). (1997). *Why people don't trust government.* Harvard University Press.

Nyhan, B., & Reifler, J. (2010). When corrections fail: The persistence of political misperceptions. *Political Behavior, 32*(2), 303–330.

Obama, M. (2021). *Becoming.* Crown.

Ogujiuba, K., Obi, K., & Dike, E. (2011). Poverty, social structure, wealth distribution and markets: Understanding the nexus. *Economics and Finance Review, 1*(6), 01–11.

Onyango, V. C. (2023). Reflections on the robbers cave experiment: Finding lessons on political conflict, racism, xenophobia, and business environments. *American Journal of Human Psychology, 1*(1), 34–38.

Ortner, S. B. (2003). *New Jersey dreaming: Capital, culture, and the class of '58.* Duke University Press.

Ostrander, S. (1984). *Women of the upper class.* Temple University Press.

Outley, C., Bowen, S., & Pinckney, H. (2021). Laughing while black: Resistance, coping and the use of humor as a pandemic pastime among blacks. *Leisure Sciences, 43*(1–2), 305–314.

Patterson, A. L., Delker, B. C., Musicaro, R., Byrne, C. A., & Noll, L. K. (2025). Impact of trauma recognition on recovery optimism and blame: An experimental vignette study of sluggish cognitive tempo (cognitive disengagement syndrome). *Stigma and Health.*

Paul, R., & Elder, L. (2007). Critical thinking: The art of Socratic questioning. *Journal of Developmental Education, 31*(1), 34–35.

Perry, J. C., & Bond, M. (2012). Change in defense mechanisms during long-term dynamic psychotherapy and five-year outcome. *American Journal of Psychiatry, 169*(9), 916–925. https://doi.org/10.1176/appi.ajp.2012.110.1403

Peters, W. (1987). *A class divided: Then and now.* Yale University Press.

Petrides, K. V., Frederickson, N., & Furnham, A. (2004). The role of trait emotional intelligence in academic performance and deviant behavior at school. *Personality and Individual Differences, 36,* 277–293.

Pew Research Center. (2023). *Public attitudes toward artificial intelligence and automation.* Pew Research Center. https://www.pewresearch.org/

Pino, N. W., & Meier, R. F. (1999). Gender differences in rape reporting. *Sex Roles, 40*(11), 979–990.

Plant, E. A., Hyde, J. S., Keltner, D., & Devine, P. G. (2000). The gender stereotyping of emotions. *Psychology of Women Quarterly, 24*(1), 81–92.

Pratiwi, A. M. (2018). *Women in science, technology, engineering & mathematics (STEM) education: Internalization oppression & sexual division labor a case study at department metallurgy and material engineering, University of Indonesia.* Asia-Pacific Research in Social Sciences and Humanities (APRiSH).

Purcell, M., & Glinder, K. (2022). *Teaching kids to pause, cope, and connect: Lessons for social emotional learning and mindfulness.* Free Spirit Publishing.

Rabin, R. C. (2025, January 5). Surgeon general calls for cancer warnings on alcohol. *The New York Times.* https://www.nytimes.com/2025/01/03/health/alcohol-surgeon-general-warning.html

Rassin, E. (2008). Individual differences in the susceptibility to confirmation bias. *Netherlands Journal of Psychology, 64*, 87–93. https://doi.org/10.1001/jama.2020.21332

Ries, M. (2022). The COVID-19 infodemic: Mechanism, impact, and counter-measures – A review of reviews. *Sustainability, 14*(5), 2605. https://doi.org/10.3390/su14052605

Rivers, W. H. (1918). The repression of war experience. *Proceedings of the Royal Society of Medicine, 11*(Sect_Psych), 1–20.

Robbins, M. (2024). *The let them theory: A life-changing tool that millions of people can't stop talking about.* Hay House, Inc.

Rodriguez Mosquera, P. M., Fischer, A. H., Manstead, A. S., & Zaalberg, R. (2008). Attack, disapproval, or withdrawal? The role of honour in anger and shame responses to being insulted. *Cognition and Emotion, 22*(8), 1471–1498.

Roppolo, K. (2013). Symbolic racism, history and reality: The real problem with Indian mascots. In M. Adams, W. J. Blumenfeld, C. Castaneda, H. W. Hackman, M. L. Peters, & X. Zuniga (Eds.), *Readings for diversity and social justice* (3rd ed., pp. 73–77). Routledge.

Roy, P., Ashton, L., Wang, T., Gorradini, M. G., Fraser, E. D. G., Thimmanagari, M., Tiessan, M., Balie, A., Saharan, K. M., Mohanty, A. K., & Misra, M. (2021). Evolution of drinking straws and their environmental, economic and societal implications. *Journal of Cleaner Production, 316*, 128234. https://doi.org/10.1016/j.jclepro.2021.128234

Rushdie, S. (2024). *Knife: Meditations after an attempted murder.* Random House.

Ryan, W. (1976). *Blaming the victim.* Vintage.

Ryan, W. (2010). Blaming the victim. In P. S. Rothenberg (Ed.), *Race, class and gender in the United States* (8th ed., pp. 648–658). Worth.

Ryckman, R. M. (2008). *Theories of personality* (9th ed.). Thomson Wadsworth.

Salecl, R. (2022). *A passion for ignorance: What we choose not to know and why.* Princeton University Press.

Salovey, P., & Mayer, J. D. (1990). Emotional intelligence. *Imagination, Cognition and Personality, 9*(3), 185–211. https://doi.org/10.2190/DUGG-P24E-52WK-6CDG

Samuel, L. R. (2012). *The American dream: A cultural history.* Syracuse University Press.

Sapolsky, R. M. (2004). *Why zebras don't get ulcers* (3rd ed.). Holt Paperbacks.

Scheff, T., Daniel, G. R., & Sterphone, J. (2018). Shame and a theory of war and violence. *Aggression and Violent Behavior, 39*, 109–115.

Schwartz, R. (2023). *Introduction to internal family systems.* Sounds True.

Schwartz, R., & Sweezy, M. (2020). *Internal family systems therapy* (2nd ed.). Guilford Press.

Shakespeare, W. (1992/1604). *The tragedy of Hamlet, prince of Denmark* (New Folger's ed.). Washington Square Press/Pocket Books.

Shapiro, F. (2012). *Getting past your past: Take control of your life with self-help techniques from EMDR therapy.* Rodale Press.

Sharma, N., Chakrabarti, S., & Grover, S. (2016). Gender differences in caregiving among family - Caregivers of people with mental illnesses. *World Journal of Psychiatry, 6*(1), 7–17. https://doi.org/10.5498/wjp.v6.i1.7. PMID: 27014594; PMCID: PMC4804270

Sharon-David, H., & Tenenbaum, G. (2017). The effectiveness of exercise interventions on coping with stress: Research synthesis. *Studies in Sport Humanities, 22*, 19–29.

Sheerin, J. (2018, October 26). *Matthew Shepard: The murder that changed America.* BBC. https://www.bbc.com/news/world-us-canada-45968606

Sherif, M. (1988). *The robbers cave experiment: Intergroup conflict and cooperation* [Orig. pub. as Intergroup conflict and group relations]. Wesleyan University Press.

Shields, S. A. (1975). Functionalism, Darwinism, and the psychology of women: A study in social myth. *American Psychologist*, 739–754. https://doi.org/10.1037/h0076948

Silver, W. S., & Mitchell, T. R. (1990). The status quo tendency in decision making. *Organizational Dynamics, 18*(4), 34–46.

Smart, C. M., & Segalowitz, S. J. (2017). Respond, don't react: The influence of mindfulness training on performance monitoring in older adults. *Cognitive, Affective, & Behavioral Neuroscience, 17*, 1151–1163.

Smidt, K. E., & Suvak, M. K. (2015). A brief, but nuanced, review of emotional granularity and emotion differentiation research. *Current Opinion in Psychology, 3*, 48–51.

Smith, J. L., & Huntoon, M. (2014). Women's bragging rights: Overcoming modesty norms to facilitate women's self-promotion. *Psychology of Women Quarterly, 38*(4), 447–459.

Sznycer, D., Sell, A., & Dumont, A. (2022). How anger works. *Evolution and Human Behavior, 43*(2), 122–132.

Spelman, E. V. (1988). *Inessential woman: Problems of exclusion in feminist thought.* Beacon Press.

Spiro, R. J., Feltovich, P. J., Jacobson, M. J., & Coulson, R. L. (2012). Cognitive flexibility, constructivism, and hypertext: Random access instruction for advanced knowledge acquisition in ill-structured domains. In *Constructivism in education* (pp. 85–107). Routledge.

Spivey, S. E. (2005). Distancing and solidarity as resistance to sexual objectification in a nude dancing bar. *Deviant Behavior*, *26*(5), 417–437. https://doi.org/10.1080/016396290931731

Steinbock, B. (1978). Speciesism and the idea of equality. *Philosophy*, *53*(204), 247–256. https://doi.org/10.1017/S0031819100016582. S2CID 170331649

Staub, E. (2006). Reconciliation after genocide, mass killing, or intractable conflict: Understanding the roots of violence, psychological recovery, and steps toward a general theory. *Political Psychology*, *27*(6), 867–894. https://doi.org/10.1111/j.1467-9221.2006.00541.x

Suler, J. (2004). The online disinhibition effect. *Cyberpsychology & Behavior*, *7*(3), 321–326.

Sumeracki, M., & Kaminske, A. N. (2024). *The psychology of memory*. Routledge.

Sutton, J. (2021, August 23). *Defense mechanism worksheets: 10 tools for practitioners*. PositivePsychology.com.

Suyemoto, K. L., & Hochman, A. L. (2021). "Taking the empathy to an activist state": Ally development as continuous cycles of critical understanding and action. *Research in Human Development*, *18*(1–2), 105–148. https://doi.org/10.1080/15427609.2021.1928453

Sweller, J. (1988). Cognitive load during problem-solving: Effects on learning. *Cognitive Science*, *12*(2), 257–285.

Tajfel, H., & Turner, J. C. (1979). An integrative theory of intergroup conflict. In W. G. Austin & S. Worchel (Eds.), *The social psychology of intergroup relations* (pp. 33–47). Brooks-Cole.

Tatro, S. E., & Marshall, J. M. (1982). Regression: A defense mechanism for the dying older adult. *Journal of Gerontological Nursing*, *8*(1), 20–22.

Tesser, A. (1988). Toward a self-evaluation maintenance model of social behavior. In L. Berkowitz (Ed.), *Advances in experimental social psychology, Vol. 21. Social psychological studies of the self: Perspectives and programs* (pp. 181–227). Academic Press.

Thompson, B. W. (1994). *A hunger so wide and so deep: American women speak out on eating problems*. University of Minnesota Press.

Thornton, S. (2016). Fear of change: Helping children and young people cope. *British Journal of School Nursing*, *11*(6), 299–301. https://doi.org/10.12968/bjsn.2016.11.6.299

Tiggemann, M., & Policy, J. (2010). Upward and downward: Social comparison processing of thin idealized media images. *Psychology of*

Women Quarterly, 34(3), 356–364. https://doi.org/10.1111/j.1471-6402.2010.01581.x

Troncale, J. (2014). *Your lizard brain: The limbic system and brain functioning.* Psychology Today.

Tyerman, A., & Spencer, C. (1983). A critical test of the Sherifs' robber's cave experiments: Intergroup competition and cooperation between groups of well-acquainted individuals. *Small Group Behavior, 14*(4), 515–531.

Twiss, M., Turchmanovych-Hienkel, N., & Corrigan, P. (2025). The benefits and unintended consequences of anti-stigma campaigns. In M. C. Yzer & J. T. Siegel (Eds.), *The Handbook of Mental Health Communication* (pp. 347–359). Wiley.

Vaillant, G. E. (1992). *Ego mechanisms of defense: A guide for clinicians and researchers.* American Psychiatric Publishing.

Vallone, R. P., Ross, L., & Lepper, M. R. (1985). The hostile media phenomenon: Biased perception and perceptions of media bias in coverage of the Beirut massacre. *Journal of Personality and Social Psychology, 49*(3), 577–585.

van de Ven, N. (2017). Envy and admiration: Emotion and motivation following upward social comparison. *Cognition and Emotion, 31*(1), 193–200. https://doi.org/10.1080/02699931.2015.1087972

Van der Kolk, B. (2014). *The body keeps the score: Brain, mind, and body in the healing of trauma.* Penguin Books.

Vanderpool, M. (2021). Body science of survivorship: Mapping the neurological impacts of interlocking systems of oppression and co-designing equitable solutions through movement and breath. In C. Hagan (Ed.), *Practicing yoga as resistance: Voices of color in search of freedom* (pp. 122–138). Routledge.

Viera, J. S. C., Marques, M. R. C., Nazareth, M. C., Jimenez, P. C., & Castro, I. B. (2020). On replacing single-use plastic with so-called biodegradable ones: The case with straws. *Environmental Science & Policy, 106*, 177–181. https://doi.org/10.1016/j.envsci.2020.02.007

Vinney, C. (2019). *Status quo bias: What it means and how it affects your behavior.* ThoughtCo. https://www.thoughtco.com/status-quo-bias-4172981

Volkan, V. D. (2004). *Blind trust: Large groups and their leaders in times of crisis and terror.* Pitchstone Publishing.

Vygotsky, L. S., & Cole, M. (1978). *Mind in society: Development of higher psychological processes.* Harvard University Press.

Wade, C., & Tavris, C. (2012). *Invitation to psychology* (5th ed.). Prentice Hall.

Wang, X., Hegde, S., Son, C., Keller, B., Smith, A., & Sasangohar, F. (2020). Investigating mental health of US college students during the COVID-19 pandemic: Cross-sectional survey study. *Journal of Medical Internet Research, 22*(9), e22817.

Westen, D. (2007). *The political brain: The role of emotion in deciding the fate of the nation.* PublicAffairs.

Whitehead, A. L., & Perry, S. L. (2018). Unbuckling the Bible belt: A state-level analysis of religious factors and google searches for porn. *The Journal of Sex Research, 55*(3), 273–283. https://doi.org/10.1080/00224499.2017.1278736

Whitford, D. M. (2017). *The curse of Ham in the early modern era: The Bible and the justifications for slavery.* Routledge.

Wilson, G. T. (1988). Alcohol and anxiety. *Behaviour Research and Therapy, 26*(5), 369–381.

Wilson, K. J. (2006). *When violence begins at home: A comprehensive guide to understanding and ending domestic abuse.* Hunter House.

Wilson, L. C., & Miller, K. E. (2016). Meta-analysis of the prevalence of unacknowledged rape. *Trauma, Violence, & Abuse, 17*(2), 149–159.

Wilson, W. J. (2010). *More than just race: Being Black and poor in the inner city (Issues of our time).* W.W. Norton & Company.

Wing, D. M. (1995). Transcending alcoholic denial. *Journal of Nursing Scholarship, 27*(2), 121–126.

Wing Sue, D., Torino, G. C., Capodilupo, C. M., Rivera, D. P., & Lin, A. I. (2009). How White faculty perceive and react to difficult dialogues on race: Implications for education and training. *The Counseling Psychologist, 37*(8), 1090–1115.

Wong, C. S., & Law, K. S. (2002). The effects of leader and follower emotional intelligence on performance and attitude. *The Leadership Quarterly, 13*, 243–274.

Wright, S. E. (1993). Blaming the victim, blaming society or blaming the discipline: Fixing responsibility for poverty and homelessness 1. *Sociological Quarterly, 34*(1), 1–16.

Yamato, G. (1990). Something about the subject makes it hard to name. In L. Richardson, V. Taylor, & N. Whittier (Eds.), *Feminist frontiers IV* (pp. 28–30). McGraw Hill.

Yap, A., & Ichikawa, J. (2024). Defensiveness and identity. *Journal of the American Philosophical Association, 10*, 261–280.

Yilmaz, E. (2024, September 27). *Minimizing: Definition in psychology, theory & examples*. Berkeley Well-Being Institute. https://www.berkeleywellbeing.com/minimizing.html#:~:text=In%20other%20words%2C%20minimizing%20is,denying%20or%20dismissing%20its%20significance.&text=Minimization%20can%20be%20a%20conscious,that%20he%20was%20merely%20joking

Young, I. M. (2008). Five faces of oppression. In J. P. Jones, III, H. J. Nast, & S. M. Tuathail (Eds.), *Geographic thought: A praxis perspective* (pp. 55–71). Routledge.

Yurdakul, D., & Atik, D. (2016). Coping with poverty through internalization and resistance: The role of religion. *Journal of Macromarketing, 36*(3), 321–336. https://doi.org/10.1177/0276146715609658

Zaccaro, S. J., LaPort, K., & José, I. (2013). The attributes of successful leaders: A performance requirements approach. In M. G. Rumsey (Ed.), *The Oxford handbook of leadership* (pp. 11–36). Oxford University Press.

Index

A

accountability, 27, 96
  and defensiveness, 94, 103
  shared responsibility, 34
affect regulation, 24, 36, 84, 94, 124
anger, 22, 85–87, 135
  as core emotion, 28–31, 63
  cultural rules about, 68
  misattribution of, 65, 72, 90–91, 101
  see also core emotions
anxiety, 14, 15, 17, 24, 32, 66, 84, 147
  and avoidance, 65, 70, 88, 90, 91, 93
  as inhibitory emotion, 28–29, 63, 81
  see also fear
armor (metaphor), 2, 5
attachment, 54, 157
avoidance, 65–67
  as defense mechanism, 85

B

belief in a just world, 47–51, 73, 75
bias, 119, 144, 150
  and defensiveness, 52–54
  implicit, 36, 47
  in-group, 37–41, 43–45, 144
  see also stereotypes
blame, 26, 31, 58, 72–77
  externalizing, 78–79, 100, 103–104, 118, 144
  internalizing, 26–27, 33
body, 3, 27
  sensations as emotional cues, 56, 81, 112, 116
  threat responses, 113–114, 131, 133

C

Change Triangle (Hendel), 28–31, 38, 58, 63, 70, 81
  core emotions, 28–29, 63, 81
  inhibitory emotions, 28–29, 63, 66, 81
  openhearted state (8 Cs), 28–29, 63, 112, 157
classroom dynamics
  difficult dialogues, 13, 24
  student defensiveness, 3, 13, 22, 35, 39, 62–63, 65, 101, 106, 123, 135
cognitive dissonance, 26, 63, 96, 102

Transforming Defensiveness: A Guidebook for Rewriting Our Stories & Reclaiming Connection, First Edition. Andrea L. Dottolo.
© 2026 John Wiley & Sons, Inc. All rights reserved, including rights for text and data mining and training of artificial intelligence technologies or similar technologies.
Published 2026 by John Wiley & Sons, Inc.

compassion, 29, 63, 81, 91, 100, 135, 139, 157
conflict, 14, 17, 26, 27, 72, 78, 92, 93, 97, 101, 103–104, 122, 142
connection, 5, 29, 105, 121, 123, 146
coping, 24, 114
   vs. defensiveness, 32
   emotion-focused, 101
   problem-focused, 32
core emotions, 28–29, 63, 81
   anger, 26, 28–29, 31, 63, 65, 68, 85–87, 91, 105, 140, 154
   disgust, 28, 58, 63
   excitement, 28, 113
   fear, 8, 14, 22, 26–27, 53–57, 63, 67, 68, 80, 85, 135, 147
   joy, 3, 28
   sadness, 8, 26, 28, 31, 62–63, 65, 68, 85, 88, 105, 132, 135
   sexual excitement, 28
culture, 6, 9, 23, 31, 45–46, 49, 63, 86, 88, 98, 125, 157
   and defensiveness, 37–38, 47, 73, 77
   emotional rules, 28, 89
   norms, 13, 52, 68, 70, 129

D

defense mechanisms, 91, 94, 101, 107
   conscious *vs.* unconscious, 49, 74, 83
   costs and benefits, 74, 99, 100
   definition, 14
   protective function, 61, 67, 72, 98, 106
defensiveness, 25
   conscious *vs.* unconscious, 15, 57, 90
   cultural level, 30, 43, 46, 72

   definition, 13, 15
   in digital spaces, 140–142, 147–152
   individual level, 26, 30, 49, 85, 88
   in political contexts, 143–146
   relational level, 39, 40
   as response to threat, 14, 23
   systems level, 30, 43
   transformation of, 111–125, 150–156
denial, 61–65, 74, 103, 130–131, 138
discomfort, 4, 6, 26, 52, 70, 92, 96, 97, 99, 103, 157
   vs. danger, 36
   as learning signal, 14, 16, 17, 20
discrimination, 8, 43–47, 75, 109, 117–118, 121, 124
distancing, 95–98

E

education, 7, 10, 24, 42, 45, 74, 86, 98, 120, 125, 153
emotional granularity, 24, 88
emotional intelligence, 24, 101, 114, 125, 157
emotions, 3, 14, 16, 20, 24, 27, 31–32, 37, 63, 65, 68, 72, 78, 80, 93, 94, 96, 105–108, 113, 135
   core, 28, 63, 66, 81
   inhibitory, 29, 57, 63, 66, 72, 81
empathy, 10, 21, 105, 111, 124, 137, 141, 156
exercises, 32, 47, 76, 82, 89, 96, 122, 124–126, 149, 154
   reflective writing, 38, 43, 46, 53, 56, 64, 66, 69, 71, 77, 80, 87, 99, 102, 104, 109, 115, 116, 136, 142, 145, 152
   scenario analysis, 33, 43, 53, 71, 79, 82, 84, 91, 93, 94, 107, 133, 138

externalizing, 26–27, 33, 58, 78, 106
   anger and blame, 58, 78
   definition, 26

F

fear, 3, 8, 14, 22, 26–28, 53–57, 63, 67–68, 72, 80, 85, 92, 97, 113, 125, 144, 147
   as core emotion, 28, 105, 135, 136
   cultural amplification of, 49, 80, 118, 144, 150
fight / flight / freeze / fawn, 17–20

G

gender, 3–5, 8, 41, 42, 49
   cultural rules, 31, 62, 68, 88
   defensiveness around, 8, 14, 24
   emotional expression, 62, 153
group dynamics, 10, 122
guilt, 26, 57, 63, 65, 67, 70, 78, 92–94, 102, 103, 135
   as inhibitory emotion, 28–29

H

humor, 21, 121, 132
   as defense mechanism, 107–109

I

identity, 12–13, 21, 41, 43, 97, 143
implicit bias, 47
ingroup bias, 37–41, 43–44
institutions, 9, 24, 30, 40, 45, 85, 153
internalizing, 26–27, 33, 58, 106
intersectionality, 41–43, 110

L

language, 7, 10, 111
learning outcomes, 25
lizard brain (limbic system), 22, 29, 62, 83, 111–112, 114

M

minimization, 67–69
myths about defensiveness, 129–138

N

narrative, 60, 147–148
neuroscience, 21–23

O

openhearted state (8 Cs), 28–29

P

power, 30–31, 41–42, 46, 50, 52, 58, 73, 75, 88, 95, 118–119, 147
privilege, 31, 39, 75, 104, 119, 124
projection, 78–80, 90, 103

R

race, 5, 8, 13–14, 20, 24, 35, 41, 108
rationalization, 70–72, 109
reflection, 77, 82, 85, 98, 100, 103, 104, 107, 109, 120, 125, 134, 146, 154
relationships, 5–9, 16, 21, 23, 25, 27, 37, 45, 73, 88, 91, 97, 105–106, 111, 117, 119, 156
religious or biological "law," 98–100

S

safety, 6, 21, 45, 81, 96, 117, 118, 121, 132, 140, 151
shame, 26, 28–29, 57–59, 62, 63, 65, 67, 72, 81, 96, 103, 118, 132, 135
silence, 5, 36, 74, 139
stereotypes, 44–46, 68, 75
  see also bias
systems, 30–31, 60, 75–76, 78, 85, 88, 90, 96, 106

T

threat, 6, 13–22, 26, 37, 67, 86, 130, 147
trauma, 21, 56, 80–82, 113, 157

U

undoing, 93–95

W

wizard brain (prefrontal cortex), 22, 29, 62, 83–84, 111–112
workplace dynamics, 9–11, 33, 45, 122, 125, 153

People & Key Theorists

A
Aronson, Leon – cognitive dissonance, 26, 63, 96, 102

B
Bandura, Albert – social learning theory, 103, 124

C
Collins, Patricia Hill – intersectionality, 41

F
Festinger, Leon – cognitive dissonance, 26, 50
Folkman, Susan – coping theory, 32
Freud, Anna – defensiveness, 92
Freud, Sigmund – defense mechanisms; iceberg metaphor, 7, 15, 30, 62, 78, 80, 83, 91, 93, 105

H
Harro, Bobbie – awareness and social change, 23, 117

Hendel
Hendel, Hilary Jacobs – Change Triangle, 28–31, 81, 88, 96, 112, 118
Herman, Judith – trauma, 80

L
Lazarus, Richard – coping theory, 32

M
Mayer, John – emotional intelligence, 24

R
Rushdie, Salman – ideological threat and violence, 21–22
Ryan, William – blaming the victim, 74

S
Salovey, Peter – emotional intelligence, 24
Schwartz, Richard – Internal Family Systems; 8 Cs, 29

V
Van der Kolk, Bessel – trauma and nervous system, 22, 80, 113

Transforming Defensiveness: A Guidebook for Rewriting Our Stories & Reclaiming Connection, First Edition. Andrea L. Dottolo.
© 2026 John Wiley & Sons, Inc. All rights reserved, including rights for text and data mining and training of artificial intelligence technologies or similar technologies.
Published 2026 by John Wiley & Sons, Inc.

Printed and bound by CPI Group (UK) Ltd, Croydon, CR0 4YY
22/04/2026

14866778-0001